Your Theological
Last Will and Testament

Your Theological
Last Will and Testament

Using Martin Luther's *Theological Last Will and Testament* to Pass Faith on to Our Children

Wesley C. Telyea

RESOURCE *Publications* · Eugene, Oregon

YOUR THEOLOGICAL LAST WILL AND TESTAMENT
Using Martin Luther's *Theological Last Will and Testament* to Pass
Faith on to Our Children

Resource Publications
An Imprint of Wipf and Stock Publishers
199 W. 8th Ave., Suite 3
Eugene, OR 97401

www.wipfandstock.com

ISBN 13: 978-1-62564-526-5

Manufactured in the U.S.A.

To my wife Emilee, who followed me to the ends of the earth, Berkeley, California, as I pursued more education, and for all the support she gave to me as I wrote this book. Without her support and wisdom, I would have given up long before its completion.

For what shall I say? How shall I complain? I am still living, writing, preaching, and lecturing daily; [and] yet there are found such spiteful men, not only among the adversaries, but also false brethren that profess to be on our side, as dare to cite my writings and doctrine directly against myself, and let me look on and listen, although they know well that I teach otherwise, and as wish to adorn their venom with my labor, and under my name to [deceive and] mislead the poor people. [Good God!] Alas! What first will happen when I am dead?

—MARTIN LUTHER, *THE SMALCALD ARTICLES*, PREF-ACE

Contents

Preface

I FELL IN LOVE with *The Book of Concord* during my last year of undergraduate work at Pacific Lutheran University in Tacoma, Washington. At the time I was writing my capstone thesis,[1] which was a comparison of Martin Luther's views on free will, found in *The Bondage of the Will*, with the views that would become Lutheran orthodoxy in *The Book of Concord*. To say I know exactly what it was about this topic that led me to fall in love with *The Book of Concord* would be a lie. All I can tell you with confidence is that something about this book attracted me to it.

Maybe it was the way the documents in *The Book of Concord* so concisely and accessibly communicated the biblical truth that excited me. Or maybe my attraction to the confessions had to do with my never having heard about this book, despite having grown up in a Lutheran home, and so when I finally learned of it I ate it like someone who had been starved. Then again, maybe the Holy Spirit dropped this book into my lap just at the time I needed it the most: before seminary. Whatever the case may be, since the fall

1. At PLU one of the graduation requirements for religion majors was to a write a capstone paper. The hope of the religion department was that its students would have to use all of the skills they had learned during their time in the program to write a scholarly paper.

of 2005, *The Book of Concord* has played a tremendous role in shaping my theological point of view and who I am as a pastor. As a matter of fact, it is safe to say my identity as a pastor has been more influenced only by scripture itself.

With this in mind, when I was asked in the fall of 2011 to lead a men's retreat for the congregation that had just called me, Saint Andrew's Lutheran Church in Bellevue, Washington, my mind instantly went to doing something focused on one of the confessional documents found in *The Book of Concord*. Why? Why wouldn't I want to lead a retreat on one of these documents? They are foundational for me, I am passionate about them, and by and large they tend to be forgotten documents for many people in the Evangelical Lutheran Church in America. It was out of this men's retreat that this book was born.

Briefly, I would like to say a few words about why I chose a confessional document and not a book from the Bible as a topic. Bible study is important. In fact there are few things that are as important as studying the Word of God, and I strongly encourage everyone to make it common practice to read scripture daily. With that said, I chose to do this retreat on one of the confessional documents for two primary reasons. First, we seem to have forgotten *The Book of Concord* and what it means to say we believe, teach, and confess certain tenets of the faith. Doing a retreat on a confessional document gave me the opportunity to explore how what we read in God's Holy Word is made manifest in what we believe, teach, and confess. It also gave me the opportunity say, "Because of what we read in scripture, we believe, teach, and confess x, y, z." In other words, the retreat offered the opportunity to make this confession that was so important to my theological heritage our confession today.

Second, for many people, reading scripture is like trying to put together a difficult word puzzle. It's confusing and hard, and leads many people to simply give up. For years my own father had told me how he had given up trying to understand what Scripture was saying. The confessions have something to offer all people, but especially people like my father who feel as though they are lost when they read the Bible. You see, the confessions are like a cheat sheet in that they help you put the puzzle together. I heard the Rev. Dr. Robert Kolb once use the analogy that the Bible is like pieces of a puzzle, and the confessions are like the picture of the puzzle on the box. Just as most of us use the picture on the box to arrive at the end product of the puzzle, the confessions help us in arriving at the end product of scripture: Christ for you. Is the picture necessary? No. Does the picture help? Yes! It was for these reasons that I chose to lead a retreat on a confessional document.

Now you are probably also wondering, "Why the Smalcald Articles (SA)? Why not the better known Augsburg Confession (AC)?" I know the men at the retreat I led had this confession. I chose the SA for two reasons. First, the SA are arguably the least known of the confessional documents, whereas the AC is arguably the best known confessional document other than Luther's catechisms. By choosing to focus on the SA, I wanted to shed light on a neglected piece of Lutheran heritage that has great relevance for today, especially given that church attendance is declining.

Second, and this reason piggybacks on the first, in my opinion the SA, while being neglected, probably speak more clearly to us today than the other documents. What I mean is that Luther, at the request of Elector John Frederick, wrote SA as a theological last will and testament. It was theological, confessional, and a means by which to pass down the essence of the faith. Growing up in the Pacific Northwest, I certainly saw the efforts of people to pass things down, mainly clean forest and habitats, but rarely do I see folks make an effort to pass down the essence of our faith. Yet, passing down this faith might be the most important thing we can do for future generations. The SA begs us to answer the question of what it is we will pass down. Will it be classical, creedal Christianity? Or will it be some newfound spirituality thingy?

My point can be illustrated by the fact that the Pacific Northwest has the lowest rate of church attendance in the United States. While there are many reasons for this, one of the major factors is that people in the Pacific Northwest think of themselves as spiritual and not religious. The claim here is that they don't need to go to church because they can access God through other means. Does the SA speak to this kind of attitude? Yep! Luther writes in the third section of SA,

> And in those things which concern the spoken, outward Word, we must firmly hold that God grants His Spirit or grace to no one, except through or with the preceding outward Word, in order that we may [thus] be protected against the enthusiasts, *i.e.*, spirits who boast that they have the Spirit without and before the Word, and accordingly judge Scripture or the spoken Word, and explain and stretch it at their pleasure, as Muenzer did, and many still do at the present day, who wish to be acute judges between the Spirit and the letter, and yet know not what they say or declare.

Certainly the situation for Luther is slightly different, as he is speaking about debates with left-wing reformers who are claiming to have experienced the spirit apart from Scripture, but as you can see the claim between the left wing-reformers and those who claim to be spiritual but not religious today are very similar: they experience God in ways outside of scripture.

It is connections like these which are endlessly intriguing. Luther wrote the SA almost 500 years ago, yet the issues he was dealing with back then we are still grappling with today. As a previous mentor and professor of mine would say, "History is not a sequence of events, it's the same damn thing over and over again."

As you read through this book, answer study questions, and ponder the SA, it is my goal for you to think about your own theological last will and testament. What did you have passed down to you? How has it changed? What will it be? Why does it matter? This book will not answer all these questions. It is, however, intended to give you something to use over the course of however long you need. You can even put it down and come back to it later. Just remember that passing down the faith is one of the most important things a person can do.

The Reverend Wesley C. Telyea
Saint Andrew's Lutheran Church
Bellevue, WA 2013

Acknowledgments

THERE ARE SO MANY people whom I should acknowledge that it's hard to know where to begin. First, I would like to thank The Reverend Dr. Daniel Peterson. Dr. Peterson was the professor who opened my eyes to the confessions and taught me how to think theologically. When we met I was in my final year at PLU, and he had just finished getting his Ph.D. from the Graduate Theological Union in Berkeley, California. Were it not for the time Dr. Peterson took with me, I do not know where I would be.

Second, I owe a deep debt of gratitude to The Reverend Dr. Michael Aune and The Reverend Dr. Jane Strohl, two of my seminary professor who continued to stoke my passion for Lutheran history and theology. My many conversations with the two of them helped me learn to think more maturely and helped me to see that you can be a "thinker" in a parish setting.

Third, I would like to acknowledge those with whom I have engaged in conversation over the last few years. In particular I would like to thank a group of guys whom I spent time with in seminary. We affectionately referred to ourselves as the "back row theologians." Their conversation has been an encouragement and a spot for deep reflection.

Acknowledgments

Fourth, I would like to thank the parish I serve: Saint Andrew's Lutheran Church in Bellevue, Washington. They have welcomed my family and me with open arms and have been a spot of constant affirmation and support. Any church that allows their pastor to engage them with the Smalcald Articles is a special place. I also work with a wonderful Senior Pastor, The Reverend James N. McEachran, who is a special mentor and friend. Without Pastor McEachran, I might not ever have gotten around to writing this book.

Finally, I need to acknowledge my wife, Emilee. She really is the smartest person I know. Her encouragement is priceless, and her support unwavering. I often refer to her as my "little theologian" because of how she can connect theological themes with everyday life. If this book is clear and understandable, it is because of her wise guidance.

1

Historical Introduction

The Basic Situation

HISTORICAL INTRODUCTIONS ARE AT times difficult to put together, because they assume history has a starting point. Take, for example, the American Civil War. When did it begin? Did it begin when Fort Sumter was bombed, or did it start at some point prior in the halls of Congress? You could probably make an equally convincing argument for either, depending on your point of view. When one studies the SA, the same kind of ambiguity concerning the impetus for its creation surrounds it, because while the SA finds its beginning in late 1536/early 1537, the grounds for this document were laid many years prior.

One good starting point for the SA, and the starting point I would like to use, is November of 1518. This is when Luther made his first public appeal for a general council.[1]

1. A general council is a meeting between the "bigwigs" of the church in which matters of doctrine are decided. The equivalent of a

Remember, Luther's writings were causing troubles that needed to be addressed. This council would examine possible reforms within the church.[2] Although no council was at first called, Luther and the other reformers continued to make appeals for a general council throughout the early years of the reformation. This is evident in the preface of the AC, where Philip Melanchthon, its author, makes a number of requests.[3]

Now it is important to note that when Luther and the other reformers called for a council, they called for a free council. What this means is simple. Luther and the other reformers wanted a council that made its decisions based only on Scripture. Those who study Luther will note that Luther was attacking papal infallibility here, and this was certainly a theme throughout Luther's career. However, I think it's more important to note that the driving force behind this was Luther's concern for the individual's conscience. You see, as Luther was going about the reform, the basis of his concern that drove his effort was that God's Word should be clearly heard in order that there be no question in an individual's mind that might torment him. Calling for a free council was part of allowing God's Word to have the final say.

It wouldn't be until 1527 that, during the Recess of Regensburg and the two diets of Speyer (1526/9), the Roman

---

general council in the ELCA could be seen as the churchwide assembly that takes place every two years and makes decisions regarding church polity and doctrine.

2. William R. Russell, *Luther's Theological Testament: The Schmalkald Articles* (Minneapolis, Minnesota: Augsburg Fortress, 1995), 15.

3. Robert Kolb, Timothy J. Wengert, and James Schaffer, "Augsburg Confession," in *The Book of Concord: The Confessions of the Evangelical Lutheran Church*, ed. Robert Kolb and Timothy J. Wengert, trans. Charles Arand et al. (Minneapolis: Fortress Press, 2000), 34:21-4.

Catholic delegates would finally acknowledge a need for a general council, and even then there were questions regarding whether or not it would be a free council.[4] Furthermore, "acknowledge" is the key word here because although they recognized this need, they did not act on it, and as a matter of fact it would still be a matter of time before any action would be taken. However, the need was recognized.

At the diet of Augsburg in 1530, things seemed to begin and gather momentum as Emperor Charles V responded to the reformer's request for a council by promising to encourage the pope to convoke one.[5] Although nothing would happen for another five years, in 1535 Pope Paul III would send a papal legate to Germany to inquire about the reformer's[6] attitudes toward a council.[7] This papal legate would eventually meet privately with both Luther and his elector, John Fredrick. As one might expect, the reaction of the reformers was guarded and skeptical. Requests and promises had been made in the past, and nothing had come from them. Why would this time be different? What had changed?

More importantly, it should be quickly noted that Rome had tried to deal with Luther early during the Reformation and had failed. In light of Rome's intervention,

4. Mark U. Edwards, Jr., *Luther's Last Battles: Politics and Polemics 1531-46* (Ithaca: Cornell University Press, 1983), 74.

5. Russell, 15.

6. It would be fair to say that these reformers are Lutherans; however, I am refraining from doing so in this article because the reformers didn't see themselves at Lutherans. The reformers saw themselves as well within the boundaries of Catholic Christianity. As a matter of fact one could probably say that the reformers saw themselves as within the boundaries of Catholic Christianity, and the Roman Catholic Church of their day as outside the boundaries of Catholic Christianity.

7. Edwards, 77.

the Schmalkald League was formed. The Schmalkald League was a group of German princes that joined to secure themselves against a possible attack by either papal or imperial forces.[8] What's important to understand for the history of the SA is that there were theological issues at work here that ran alongside political issues. Keep in mind that at this point in history there was little distinction between church and state. In other words, at this time in history the boundary between the church and the state was decidedly not well defined.

Finally, in June of 1536, Pope Paul III called a general council to meet in Mantua in May of 1537.[9] Shortly after calling the council, Pope Paul III began what can only be called an offensive in hopes of persuading the German princes and theologians to attend.[10] It shouldn't be surprising that Pope Paul III would have to work so hard to get the reformers to attend. After all, the reformers were skeptical when they had first heard about it the previous year. Come to find out their skepticism was well founded: this general council never met. Due to ecclesiastical and international politics, the council was delayed until 1545 and was what we now know as the famous Council of Trent.[11]

Opinions about this delay can be read in the preface of SA where Luther writes, "Pope Paul III called a council to meet at Mantua last year"; obviously Luther wrote the preface after the council was supposed to meet, "around

---

8. Russell, 17.

9. Robert Kolb, Timothy J. Wengert, and James Schaffer, "The Smalcald Articles: Editors' Introduction to the Smalcald Articles," in *The Book of Concord: The Confessions of the Evangelical Lutheran Church*, ed. Robert Kolb and Timothy J. Wengert, trans. Charles Arand et al. (Minneapolis, Minnesota: Fortress Press, 2000), 295.

10. Ibid.

11. Ibid.

Pentecost. Afterward he moved it from Mantua, so that it is still not known where he intends to hold it, or whether he can hold it. We on our side had to prepare for the eventuality that, whether summoned to the council or not, we would be condemned.[12]" Here is the key to understanding the historical background of the SA. While it was unknown whether a council would happen, the reformers needed a game plan in the case a council did take place. One must always be prepared so as not to look like a fool.

This led the reformers, after Pope Paul III called for a council in 1536, to meet in Schmalkalden during February of 1537 to prepare for the possibility of a council. Why prepare for a council that no one thought would actually convene? Russell notes two important reasons. First, the reformers had been appealing for a council for years; if they failed to take the calling of the council seriously and the council did in fact convene, their request would look like some kind of ploy. At the heart of this back and forth about whether or not to attend a possible council lay the truth one believed. If the reformers believed that what they were teaching was true, then they should have no worry about a council. However, if the reformers were bluffing, then not attending the council would call them, and their reform, out. Second, such a council was more than likely the only alternative to an armed conflict.[13] Remember, without what we think of as the separation of church and state, any conflict within the church had the potential to divide the Empire.

During the summer of 1536, leading up to this meeting at Schmalkald, the reformers advised elector John Frederick that it would be best to attend this proposed council. Frederick initially did not agree with the reformers, and he

12. Kolb, "Smalcald Articles," 297.
13. Russell, 17.

asked them to reconsider their position. Essentially Frederick tried to force his opinion on his theologians, so for the rest of 1536 these types of discussion continued to take place. Finally, in December of 1536, John Frederick went to Wittenburg with specific instructions about the development of a set of articles that should be written by Luther.[14] With this event, the SA found its beginning.

Luther's Medical Situation

The basic situation where the SA found its start now led into a consideration of Luther's medical condition. You see, while the proposed council certainly gave reason for the writing of a document like SA, Luther's health concerns provided an added motivation to get such a confession from the leading reformer written quickly. William Russell supports this thought as he notes that although most histories of the SA see the purposed general council as the major factor in its drafting, one cannot ignore Luther's health as another major factor.[15]

It is fairly well known that throughout the later years of his life Luther suffered from a number of illnesses. The 1530s were not a time of relaxation for Luther, but a time of unrest both politically and theologically, as well as in terms of his personal health. By 1535, when Pope Paul III had called a council to meet, Luther had already suffered and was suffering from a number of debilitating illnesses.

For example, in a letter Luther wrote to Philip Melanchthon dated August 29, 1535, just two months after Pope Paul III called a council, Luther writes, "Yesterday and today I have been suffering from diarrhea, and my body has

14. Russell, 18-9.
15. Russell, 24.

been weakened so that I cannot sleep and have no appetite, and we have nothing to drink. I hope to feel better tomorrow. In the last two days I have had fifteen bowel movements.[16]" In another entry dated October 28, 1535, Luther noted that he was suffering from a bad cold and cough.[17]

While on one hand we can look at these health issues and think "What's the big deal with diarrhea and a cold?", on the other hand we have to remember that this was the sixteenth century. Medical standards have come a long way in the past 500 years, and frankly it was these sorts of things that compromised people's health. It also behooves us to remember that the medical community at this time wasn't always the most reliable and often relied on myths to cure people.

In 1536, Luther's health issues intensified. In January of that year, in another letter written by Luther, we learn that he suffered from a coughing and sneezing fit.[18] It was also during this time that rumors seemed to spread regarding the reformer's health. For example, we read letters from people other than Luther who are concerned about his health during this period. One letter, written to Luther by Margrave George of Brandenburg-Ansbach, reads,

> Worthy and learned, especially beloved [Martin]: Recently it has been reported to us how you have been gripped by a physical ailment from our Lord God. While you suffered this illness, we suffered as Christians with you. When we heard, in answer to our earnest inquires, that you had again received health from our Lord God, undoubtedly from God's almighty power . . . we were extremely happy. We hope that

16. LW, 50:87.
17. LW, 50:108.
18. LW, 50:128-9.

> God's almighty power will linger with you for a
> long time and you continue to receive health.[19]

Maybe even more telling about Luther's health is that from mid-December 1536 to January 14, 1537, Luther did not preach, and as Russell points out, this is the only time between 1519 and 1542 that Luther didn't preach during Christmas,[20] a season which is at the heart of this theology.[21]

If 1535 and 1536 were rough years for Luther, and indeed they were, sadly, 1537 would be even worse. In 1537 Luther suffered his worst illness: a kidney stone that almost took his life. As noted by Charles Arand, Robert Kolb, and James Nestingen, Luther was suffering from uremic poisoning, and upon releasing the urine that had built up he was so happy that he reported the incident to his wife Katherine and their friends.[22]

Are you beginning to get the picture? Throughout the 1530s Luther's health was in decline, and although he would go on to live for almost ten more years after the SA were written, at the time Luther's death seemed imminent. Given this grave situation, both John Fredrick and Luther were concerned that future generations would not know what the reform efforts were really about, or what Luther

19. WABr, 7:416, trans. William R. Russell, in Russell, 26.

20. Russell, 28. The reason Luther didn't preach at this time was that he had suffered a heart attack.

21. Luther's theology of the cross is often seen as a theology that emerges out of the Lent and Easter seasons. However, a theology of the cross has much more to do with incarnation and revelation and for that reason is better understood in light of Advent.

22. Charles P. Arand, Robert Kolb, and James A. Nestingen, *The Lutheran Confessions: History and Theology of The Book of Concord* (Minneapolis: Fortress Press, 2012), 151.

believed, or what had compelled him to take on the reform of the Church.[23]

With this history in mind, I want you to see how seriously Luther, and other nontheologians, took the handing down of the faith. It wasn't seen or understood as a trivial matter, but as something of the utmost importance. It was the faith that they knew to be true because it simply and clearly proclaimed the divinity of Jesus Christ. It was something, amazingly, they were all willing to die for! With this background, we now have the foundation from which we can build our own theological last will and testament as we journey through the SA.

23. Luther puts this nicely in the preface of the SA when he wrote, For what shall I say? How shall I complain? I am still living, writing, preaching, and lecturing daily; [and] yet there are found such spiteful men, not only among the adversaries, but also false brethren that profess to be on our side, as dare to cite my writings and doctrine directly against myself, and let me look on and listen, although they know well that I teach otherwise, and as wish to adorn their venom with my labor, and under my name to [deceive and] mislead the poor people. [Good God!] Alas! what first will happen when I am dead?

2

Confessional or Theological?

THE LAST PART OF this introduction deals with the question: what kind of document is the SA? At first this question might appear unimportant, and frankly seem to be an excuse for me to babble on about a topic that is tedious and lackluster. However, I would like to point out that while theological and confessional documents hold many things in common, they are at their core different. Theological documents tend to be academic in nature and convey timeless truths. Confessional documents, on the other hand, seek to make statements about an individual's beliefs without giving extensive attention to explanation, and they involve the Word of God interacting with a community.[1]

Another way to look at this would be to think of the distinction between what Arand, Kolb, and Nestingen call "first order discourse" and "second order discourse." First order discourse gives, and second order discourse examines, that which is given.[2] So confessional documents would be

1. Russell, 43.
2. Arand, Kolb, and Nestingen, 77.

an example of first order discourse because these types of documents give a statement of what a person believes. An example of second order discourse would be a theological document because it examines the validity of the statement of beliefs a person has given. Clearly, each of these documents/discourses has its merits, but each has a different goal. For readers of Luther's SA, being able to note what Luther is attempting to do will help make the SA more accessible.

So, are the SA confessional or theological in nature? At the end of the SA Luther writes, "These are the articles on which I must stand, and, God willing, shall stand even to my death; and I do not know how to change or to yield anything in them. If any one wishes to yield anything, let him do it at the peril of his conscience." Luther also mentions in the preface that he published these articles in preparation for the possibility of a council, as we covered in the pervious section. Given what Luther writes in the SA in the preface and at its conclusion, it is fairly clear that Luther understood it as a theological document, because it was supposed to be a statement that could stand the test of time.

However, a closer look shows that Luther also understood this document as confessional. Luther writes the SA for a specific time and place, and yet they hold a timeless truth.[3] Notice what Luther writes in the preface:

> Nevertheless I have determined meanwhile to publish these articles in plain print, so that, should I die before there would be a Council (as I fully expect and hope, because the knaves who flee the light and shun the day take such wretched pains to delay and hinder the Council), those

3. Timothy Lull referred to Luther as an "occasional theologian." That is to say, "He wrote no single summary of his own teaching that can stand next to the greatest compends of Christian doctrine." Timothy F. Lull, ed., *Martin Luther's Basic Theological Writings,* 2nd ed. (Minneapolis: Augsburg Fortress, 2005), xix.

> who live and remain after me may have my testi-
> mony and confession to produce, in addition to
> the Confession which I have issued previously,
> whereby up to this time I have abided, and, by
> God's grace, will abide.

After all, on one hand Luther was concerned with what would happen to the Reformation after his death, and on the other hand he did not want people to view the Reformation as meandering outside the fence of acceptable Christian orthodoxy.

To summarize, the SA are both confessional and theological in nature. Why then was this discussion necessary? The necessity was due to the complexity of the situation in which Luther found himself as he wrote the SA. We are all products of our time and place, and so we act in certain ways given our time and place. Luther wrote the SA out of a number of different concerns: political, ecclesiastical, and health related. For this reason, the SA are a multifaceted document that cannot be pinned down to a certain genre. It's important to bear that in mind as we explore what this document is and how we should use it.

Given that you will be challenged at the end of this book to write your own theological last will and testament, notice how this confessional versus theological discussion holds relevance in your life. We live during a time in history when people are more connected than ever. It's not uncommon for people to travel around the world and see a number of different cultures every year! Technology alone is enabling us to do things we once only dreamed of. Your own theological last will and testament will undoubtedly be both theological and confessional. Making yourself aware of this will help you better communicate and be equipped to profess the faith that you hold so dear.

3

Understanding the Structure of the Smalcald Articles

Upon first glance, the structure of the SA can be a bit confusing. However, don't worry. You shouldn't be overwhelmed because believe it or not, the SA really are an organized document. The trick is recognizing what its three sections do and communicate. Section I concerns material that both the Protestants and the Roman Catholic Church *agreed* upon. Section II concerns those articles of faith that Luther thought the Protestants and Roman Catholic would *never find agreement* on. Section III concerns those articles of faith regarding which *common ground might be possible.* It's that simple. Now within this basic structure, Luther added certain articles of faith and theological issues. Below is a detailed outline.

Section I:

(Confession of ancient Trinitarian doctrine—what both parties publically agreed upon.)

Your Theological Last Will and Testament

Section II:

The First Article

Luther's teaching on what he viewed as the heart of biblical teaching (the office and work of Jesus Christ, or our redemption) and saw no hope for agreement on.

The Second Article

Concerning the Invocation of Saints

The Third Article

The Fourth Article

Section III:

(Doctrinal topics upon which Luther hoped parties could find common formulation of biblical truth.)

[1:] Concerning Sin

[2:] Concerning the Law

[3:] Concerning Repentance

Concerning the False Penance of the Papists

[4:] Concerning the Gospel

[5:] Concerning Baptism

Concerning Infant Baptism

[6:] Concerning the Sacrament of the Altar

[7:] Concerning the Keys

[8:] Concerning Confession

[9:] Concerning Excommunication

[10:] Concerning Ordination and Vocation

[11:] Concerning the Marriage of Priests

[12:] Concerning the Church

[13:] How a Person Is Justified and Concerning Good Works

[14:] Concerning Monastic Vows

[15:] Concerning Human Regulations

What is nice about the structure of the SA is how it supplies a template for you to use as you draft your own theological last will and testament. Certainly yours will not be exactly like the SA. You might have different topics in different sections, but that's what nice about writing your own—t's yours! As you now begin to read and reflect on the SA, ask yourself where you might place the topics Luther brings up, and whether you might add or take out certain topics.

4

Smalcald Articles Preface

SA Preface Reflection

MARTIN LUTHER'S PREFACE TO the SA is, to a certain degree, its most colorful and fun-to-read section. In it Luther seems to outright poke fun at his opponents, calling into question the sincerity of the proposed council and its legitimacy. In this preface Luther almost sounds like someone who no longer takes what the papacy says seriously because he is used to hearing one thing and seeing another.

Yet, notice what Luther writes in the second paragraph of the preface about why he compiled these articles. Luther states that he wrote them "in case the Pope with his adherents should ever be *so bold as seriously and in good faith, without lying and cheating,* to hold a truly free [legitimate] Christian Council" (emphasis added). Those are fighting words. Those are the words of a man who has nothing to lose and everything to gain in his confession of faith.

Here in the preface to the SA we see Luther recounting the reasons for writing the SA, poking fun (to a certain degree) at the papacy, and laying out why he believed this confession is important. As Luther writes in the third paragraph,

> Nevertheless I have determined meanwhile to publish these articles in plain print, so that, should I die before there would be a Council (as I fully expect and hope, because the knaves who flee the light and shun the day take such wretched pains to delay and hinder the Council), those who live and remain after me may have my testimony and confession.

This was serious business for Luther. In the years prior to this Luther had shaken up the entire world with his writings and his call to reform. It wasn't just the theological field that was affected by Luther's writings; other fields, such as the political, social, and economic were affected too.

As you read this preface, keep in mind that these articles are written so that the faith, which at that point in history had been skewed, might be preserved. What was at stake here for Luther wasn't just an opportunity to be heard by the leadership in the Church, but was actually Christ! By misrepresenting any of these articles, pastors in the Church risked misrepresenting the biblical image of Christ, and in doing so robbed people of the comfort that only Christ brings. In this preface Luther sets the reader up for what is truly at stake: Christ. As you read the preface, pay attention to how Luther does this, and then reflect on how you might preface your confession.

Preface Text

1] Since Pope Paul III convoked a Council last year, to assemble at Mantua about Whitsuntide, and afterwards transferred it from Mantua, so that it is not yet known where he will or can fix it, and we on our part either had to expect that we would be summoned also to the Council or [to fear that we would] be condemned unsummoned, I was directed to compile and collect the articles of our doctrine [in order that it might be plain] in case of deliberation as to what and how far we would be both willing and able to yield to the Papists, and in what points we intended to persevere and abide to the end.

2] I have accordingly compiled these articles and presented them to our side. They have also been accepted and unanimously confessed by our side, and it has been resolved that, in case the Pope with his adherents should ever be so bold as seriously and in good faith, without lying and cheating, to hold a truly free [legitimate] Christian Council (as, indeed, he would be in duty bound to do), they be publicly delivered in order to set forth the Confession of our Faith.

3] But though the Romish court is so dreadfully afraid of a free Christian Council, and shuns the light so shamefully, that it has [entirely] removed, even from those who are on its side, the hope that it will ever permit a free Council, much less that it will itself hold one, whereat, as is just, they [many Papists] are greatly offended and have no little trouble on that account [are disgusted with this negligence of the Pope], since they notice thereby that the Pope would rather see all Christendom perish and all souls damned than suffer either himself or his adherents to be reformed even a little, and his [their] tyranny to be limited, nevertheless I have determined meanwhile to publish these articles in plain print, so that, should I die before there would be a Council (as I fully expect and hope, because the knaves who flee the light and shun the day take such wretched pains to delay and hinder the Council), those who live and remain after me may have my testimony and confession to produce, in addition to the Confession which I have issued previously, whereby up to this time I have abided, and, by God's grace, will abide.

4] For what shall I say? How shall I complain? I am still living, writing, preaching, and lecturing daily; [and] yet there are found such spiteful men, not only among the adversaries, but also false brethren that profess to be on our side, as dare to cite my writings and doctrine directly against myself, and let me look on and listen, although they know well that I teach otherwise, and as wish to adorn their venom with my labor, and under my name to [deceive and] mislead the poor people. [Good God!] Alas! what first will happen when I am dead?

5] Indeed, I ought to reply to everything while I am still living. But, again, how can I alone stop all the mouths of the devil? especially of those (as they all are poisoned) who will not hear or notice what we write, but solely exercise themselves with all diligence how they may most shamefully pervert and corrupt our word in every letter. These I let the devil answer, or at last Gods wrath, as they deserve. 6] I often think of the good Gerson, who doubts whether anything good should be [written and] published. If it is not done, many souls are neglected who could be delivered; but if it is done, the devil is there with malignant, villainous tongues without number which envenom and pervert everything, so that nevertheless the fruit [the usefulness of the writings] is prevented. 7] Yet what they gain thereby is manifest. For while they have lied so shamefully against us and by means of lies wished to retain the people, God has constantly advanced His work, and been making their following ever smaller and ours greater, and by their lies has caused and still causes them to be brought to shame.

8] I must tell a story. There was a doctor sent here to Wittenberg from France, who said publicly before us that his king was sure and more than sure, that among us there is no church, no magistrate, no married life, but all live promiscuously as cattle, and each one does as he pleases. 9] Imagine now, how will those who by their writings have instilled such gross lies into the king and other countries as the pure truth, look at us on that day before the judgment-seat of Christ? Christ, the Lord and Judge of us all, knows well that they lie and have [always] lied, His sentence they in turn, must hear; that I know certainly. God convert to repentance those who can be converted! Regarding the rest it will be said, Woe, and, alas! eternally.

10] But to return to the subject. I verily desire to see a truly Christian Council [assembled some time], in order that many matters and persons might be helped. Not that we need it, for our churches are now, through God's grace, so enlightened and equipped with the pure Word and right use of the Sacraments, with knowledge of the various callings and of right works, that we on our part ask for no Council, and on such points have nothing better to hope or expect from a Council. But we see in the bishoprics everywhere so many parishes vacant and desolate that one's heart would break, and yet neither the bishops nor canons care how the poor people live or die, for whom nevertheless Christ has died, and who are not permitted to hear Him speak with them as the true Shepherd with His sheep. 11] This causes me to shudder and fear that at some time He may send a council of angels upon Germany utterly destroying us, like

Sodom and Gomorrah, because we so wantonly mock Him with the Council.

12] Besides such necessary ecclesiastical affairs, there would be also in the political estate innumerable matters of great importance to improve. There is the disagreement between the princes and the states; usury and avarice have burst in like a flood, and have become lawful [are defended with a show of right]; wantonness, lewdness, extravagance in dress, gluttony, gambling, idle display, with all kinds of bad habits and wickedness, insubordination of subjects, of domestics and laborers, of every trade, also the exactions [and most exorbitant selling prices] of the peasants (and who can enumerate all?) have so increased that they cannot be rectified by ten Councils and twenty Diets. 13] If such chief matters of the spiritual and worldly estates as are contrary to God would be considered in the Council, they would have all hands so full that the child's play and absurdity of long gowns [official insignia], large tonsures, broad cinctures [or sashes], bishops' or cardinals' hats or maces, and like jugglery would in the mean time be forgotten. If we first had performed God's command and order in the spiritual and secular estate, we would find time enough to reform food, clothing, tonsures, and surplices. But if we want to swallow such camels, and, instead, strain at gnats, let the beams stand and judge the motes, we also might indeed be satisfied with the Council.

14] Therefore I have presented few articles; for we have without this so many commands of God to observe in the Church, the state, and the family that we can never fulfil them. What, then, is the use, or what does it profit that many decrees and statutes thereon are made in the Council, especially when these chief matters commanded of God are neither regarded nor observed? Just as though He were bound to honor our jugglery as a reward of our treading His solemn commandments under foot. But our sins weigh upon us and cause God not to be gracious to us; for we do not repent, and, besides, wish to defend every abomination.

15] O Lord Jesus Christ, do Thou Thyself convoke a Council, and deliver Thy servants by Thy glorious advent! The Pope and his adherents are done for; they will have none of Thee. Do Thou, then, help us, who are poor and needy, who sigh to Thee, and beseech Thee earnestly, according to the grace which Thou hast given us, through Thy Holy Ghost, who liveth and reigneth with Thee and the Father, blessed forever. Amen.

SA Preface Study Questions

1. Luther states in paragraph one that he was directed to collect the articles of doctrine that they were willing to yield to the Papists and those that they were unwilling to yield. If you were asked this, what would your list look like?

2. The SA are Luther's theological last will and testament. In the fourth paragraph Luther raises the question: What will happen when I am dead? He raises this question as a way of asking what would happen to the Reformation when he was gone. As you think about question number one above, and those whom you love and care about, ask yourself: what will happen to the faith legacy you hold after you are gone? Will it be carried on? Will it be skewed? Does it even matter?

3. In paragraph 10 Luther writes that while he wants to see a council called, it won't break his heart if there isn't one. His reason? Because his churches already

have what he calls the "pure Word." Nevertheless, he knows other churches do not. How can we engage others who might disagree with our above list, and yet at the same time remain loving coworkers in Christ (1Tim. 1:5)? Does Luther's preface do a good job of laying this out?

4. What are your overall impressions of this preface? How might you begin a theological last will and testament?

5

Smalcald Articles Section I

SA I Reflection

Does it strike you as odd that the first part of the SA begins not with a discussion about a given topic, for example justification or baptism, but with a pronunciation of the doctrine of the Trinity? With Luther writing this for a proposed council, why would he begin with a discussion on the doctrine of the Trinity and not with the key issues at stake? Why start with what is commonly confessed and not with the real issues? Why beat around the bush? Why waste paper on trivial matters?

Luther begins the SA with a Trinitarian confession of faith, because by doing so he demonstrates his commitment to the catholic, that is to say universal, understanding of the doctrine of the Trinity. In some respects this is Luther's way of saying, "This reformation 'thing' isn't new! I am not revolting against the established norms of classical creedal Christianity. No, as a matter of faith I am going back to classical creedal Christianity. I am reclaiming what we, at this time in the history of the church, have lost. I am not a heretic—I am the prophetic voice calling for renewal."

Luther began with this Trinitarian confession of faith because his opponents were claiming he was a heretic. How do you prove you are not a heretic? For Luther, you did this by showing how reformation fell into the boundaries of what grounded the church. What better way of doing this than through confessing the doctrine of the Trinity using creedal language?

It is also an example of how Luther saw this as a theological document. By confessing the doctrine of the trinity, Luther shows its theological importance, not only for his generation, but also for generations to come. To leave this doctrine out of a theological last will and testament and will would have been detrimental. It would have been like giving someone a house, but not the land to put the house on. What good is a theological last will and testament without the proper foundation?

Two points of interest for you as you read the first part of the SA. First, do you notice something missing? Maybe scripture? Luther does not quote scripture in the first part of the SA. Now this might appear bizarre, given Luther's emphasis on "sola scriptura"; however, Russell points out that Luther was in fact being intentional in leaving Scripture out. First, Russell writes, "According to Luther, the Scriptures speak of God as three in one. The divine revelation in the Scriptures is Trinitarian and the creeds accurately reflect this self-disclosure of God."[1] Second, Russell suggests that by not quoting scripture Luther was showing that the accusations of his being a heretic were not true; he was not doing anything new; in fact, he was in line with the

1. Russell, 64.

tradition. For these reasons, scripture is absent from this opening section.

A second point of interest can be seen when you take time to notice that the longest section of part one is section IV. Notice that this article focuses on Christ's redeeming work. Is it accidental that Christ's redeeming work is the topic of the longest article in this section, given that it was also the major issue between the reformers and Rome? Probably not. Who Christ is and what Christ does is immensely important and shapes the meat of this section. As you read, keep in mind that this section contains those topics that Luther felt the Protestants and the Roman Catholics agreed upon.

Smalcald Articles Section I Text

The First Part

Treats of the Sublime Articles Concerning the Divine Majesty, as:

  I. *That Father, Son, and Holy Ghost, three distinct persons in one divine essence and nature, are one God, who has created heaven and earth.*

 II. *That the Father is begotten of no one; the Son of the Father; the Holy Ghost proceeds from Father and Son.*

III. *That not the Father nor the Holy Ghost but the Son became man.*

IV. *That the Son became man in this manner, that He was conceived, without the cooperation of man, by the Holy Ghost, and was born of the pure, holy [and always] Virgin Mary. Afterwards He suffered, died, was buried, descended to hell, rose from the dead, ascended to heaven, sits at the right hand of God, will come to judge the quick and the dead, etc., as the Creed of the Apostles, as well as that of St. Athanasius, and the Catechism in common use for children, teach.*

Concerning these articles there is no contention or dispute, since we on both sides confess them. Therefore it is not necessary now to treat further of them.

SA I Study Questions

1. Do you find it important that Luther begins his theological last will and testament with a confession of the doctrine of the Trinity? Would you include it in your own?

2. In our modern society the doctrine of the Trinity can, and does, offend people. What might be offensive about it? Is it offensive the way Luther presents it? If you were the Pope, would you be offended by Luther's presentation?

3. Originally the last paragraph of the first part read, "Concerning these articles there is no contention or dispute, since we on both sides *believe and* confess them. Therefore it is not necessary now to treat further of them." Why do you think Luther took out the words "believe and?" Is there a difference between believing and confessing?

6

Smalcald Articles Section II

SA II Reflection

WE MIGHT DO WELL to remember how the SA are laid out: in such a way that in SA I Luther presents those things that he believes can be agreed upon by everyone involved, in SA II Luther presents those things that he believes the two parties will never agree upon, and in SA III he presents items that there is some hope of agreement on. I remind you of this because here we enter into a part of the SA that is highly polemical. In other words, this is the fun section, because this is where Luther comes to life! He has nothing to lose, so he clearly lays out his position and his confession.

A few things to note as you begin to read. First, whereas SA I contains no explicit reference to scripture, SA II is quite different. You will notice, especially in SA II, 1, that there are almost more references to Scripture than there are words. Why the shift? What has changed? Several things have changed. For example, just based on the structure of the SA we know that SA II is dealing with items that the two parties did not agree with each other about. Because of this disagreement, Luther needed to show how his understanding of the doctrine of justification was in accord with the earliest understanding. How could this be done? By appealing to scripture, because scripture predates tradition, reason, and experience. It even predates the pope!

Second, Luther begins SA II in article I with a key distinction that is made to point out why there can be no compromising with the papacy in SA II 2, 3, and 4. This distinction is made between the law and the gospel, and it sets up the hermeneutic that guides Luther and his understanding of the doctrine of justification. Russell writes, "For Luther, the language of 'the forgiveness of sin' (and, for that matter, 'justification by faith') points to the same phenomenon as 'the distinction between law and gospel.'[1] This distinction between the law and the gospel is critical because it lays out how we are to understand the office and work of Christ. The law condemns. The Gospel brings to life. The law reveals to a person their sin. The Gospel saves. The reason that the reformers and Rome were unable to agree upon the doctrine of justification is because they could not agree on the office and work of Christ. You see, if Christ has come to save a fallen humanity, then there can be nothing left for sinful people to do. If there were, according to this distinction, then Christ would lay upon sinful people a new law and not give the gospel.

After Luther laid out the distinction between the law and the gospel in SA II, 1 and called it the article upon which everything they taught stood, he used this article as his source for an attack on the mass (SA II, 2), monasteries (SA II, 3), and the papacy (SA II, 3). What we find in the SA following SA II, 1 is the application of who Jesus

1. Russell, 72.

was and what this meant for the church. Luther contended that the Church had been misusing its power because it did not understand who Jesus was/is and the implications that come from it; namely, from whence we receive the forgiveness of sin. As you read this section, I invite you to ponder how this chief article (SA II, 1) plays itself out in the other articles in SA II.

Furthermore, I invite you to consider what it is that your faith stands or falls upon. Once you're able to name it, think about why it is that particular thing. We all have something that we hold near and dear to us, but seldom do we take the time to discover what its implications are. What makes SA II so valuable is how Luther did just that. This is the heart of Luther's theological last will and testament; pay attention and allow his passion to influence yours.

Smalcald Articles Section II Text

The Second Part

Treats of the Articles which Refer to the Office and Work of Jesus Christ, or Our Redemption.

Part II, Article I: The first and chief article.

1] *That Jesus Christ, our God and Lord, died for our sins, and was raised again for our justification*, Rom. 4:25.

2] *And He alone is the Lamb of God which taketh away the sins of the world*, John 1:29; *and God has laid upon Him the iniquities of us all*, Is. 53:6.

3] *Likewise: All have sinned and are justified without merit [freely, and without their own works or merits] by His grace, through the redemption that is in Christ Jesus, in His blood*, Rom. 3:23f

4] Now, since it is necessary to believe this, and it cannot be otherwise acquired or apprehended by any work, law, or merit, it is clear and certain that this faith alone justifies us as St. Paul says, Rom. 3:28: *For we conclude that a man is justified by faith, without the deeds of the Law.* Likewise 3:26: *That He might be just, and the Justifier of him which believeth in Christ.*

5] Of this article nothing can be yielded or surrendered [nor can anything be granted or permitted contrary to the same], even though heaven and earth, and whatever will not abide, should sink to ruin. *For there is none other name under heaven, given among men whereby we must be saved*, says Peter, Acts 4:12. *And with His stripes we are healed*, Is. 53:5. And upon this article all things depend which we teach and practice in opposition to the Pope, the devil, and the [whole] world. Therefore, we must be sure concerning this doctrine, and not doubt; for otherwise all is lost, and the Pope and devil and all things gain the victory and suit over us.

Part II, Article II: Of the Mass.

1] That the Mass in the Papacy must be the greatest and most horrible abomination, as it directly and powerfully conflicts with this chief article, and yet above and before all other popish idolatries it has been the chief and most specious. For it has been held that this sacrifice or work of the Mass, even though it be rendered by a wicked [and abandoned] scoundrel, frees men from sins, both in this life and also in purgatory, while only the Lamb of God shall and must do this, as has been said above. Of this article nothing is to be surrendered or conceded, because the first article does not allow it.

2] If, perchance, there were reasonable Papists we might speak moderately and in a friendly way, thus: first, why they so rigidly uphold the Mass. For it is but a pure invention of men, and has not been commanded by God; and every invention of man we may [safely] discard, as Christ declares, Matt. 15:9: *In vain do they worship Me, teaching for doctrines the commandments of men.*

3] Secondly. It is an unnecessary thing, which can be omitted without sin and danger.

4] Thirdly. The Sacrament can be received in a better and more blessed way [more acceptable to God], (yea, the only blessed way), according to the institution of Christ. Why, then, do they drive the world to woe and [extreme] misery on account of a fictitious, unnecessary matter, which can be well obtained in another and more blessed way?

5] Let [care be taken that] it be publicly preached to the people that the Mass as men's twaddle [commentitious affair or human figment] can be omitted without sin, and that no one will be condemned who does not observe it, but that he can be saved in a better way without the Mass. I wager [Thus it will come to pass] that the Mass will then collapse of itself, not only among the insane [rude] common people, but also among all pious, Christian, reasonable, God-fearing hearts; and that the more, when they would hear that the Mass is a [very] dangerous thing, fabricated and invented without the will and Word of God.

6] Fourthly. Since such innumerable and unspeakable abuses have arisen in the whole world from the buying and selling of masses, the Mass should by right be relinquished, if for no other purpose than to prevent abuses, even though in itself it had something advantageous and good. How much more ought we to relinquish it, so as to prevent [escape] forever these horrible abuses, since it is altogether unnecessary, useless, and dangerous, and we can obtain everything by a more necessary, profitable, and certain way without the Mass.

7] Fifthly. But since the Mass is nothing else and can be nothing else (as the Canon and all books declare), than a work of men (even of wicked scoundrels), by which one attempts to reconcile himself and others to God, and to obtain and merit the remission of sins and grace (for thus the Mass is observed when it is observed at the very best; otherwise what purpose would it serve?), for this very reason it must and should [certainly] be condemned and rejected. For this directly conflicts with the chief article, which says that it is not a wicked or a godly hireling of the Mass with his own work, but the Lamb of God and the Son of God, that taketh away our sins.

8] But if any one should advance the pretext that as an act of devotion he wishes to administer the Sacrament, or Communion, to himself, he is not in earnest [he would commit a great mistake, and would not be speaking seriously and sincerely]. For if he wishes to commune in sincerity, the surest and best way for him is in the Sacrament administered according to Christ's institution. But that one administer communion to himself is a human notion, uncertain, unnecessary, yea, even prohibited. And he does not know what he is doing, because without the Word of God he obeys a false human opinion and invention. 9] So, too, it is not right (even though the matter were otherwise correct) for one to use the common Sacrament of [belonging to] the Church according to his own private devotion, and without

God's Word and apart from the communion of the Church to trifle therewith.

10] This article concerning the Mass will be the whole business of the Council. [The Council will perspire most over, and be occupied with this article concerning the Mass.] For if it were [although it would be] possible for them to concede to us all the other articles, yet they could not concede this. As Campegius said at Augsburg that he would be torn to pieces before he would relinquish the Mass, so, by the help of God, I, too, would suffer myself to be reduced to ashes before I would allow a hireling of the Mass, be he good or bad, to be made equal to Christ Jesus, my Lord and Savior, or to be exalted above Him. Thus we are and remain eternally separated and opposed to one another. They feel well enough that when the Mass falls, the Papacy lies in ruins. Before they will permit this to occur, they will put us all to death if they can.

11] *In addition to all this, this dragon's tail, [I mean] the Mass, has begotten a numerous vermin-brood of manifold idolatries.*

12] First, purgatory. Here they carried their trade into purgatory by masses for souls, and vigils, and weekly, monthly, and yearly celebrations of obsequies, and finally by the Common Week and All Souls' Day, by soul-baths so that the Mass is used almost alone for the dead, although Christ has instituted the Sacrament alone for the living. Therefore purgatory, and every solemnity, rite, and commerce connected with it, is to be regarded as nothing but a specter of the devil. For it conflicts with the chief article [which teaches] that only Christ, and not the works of men, are to help [set free] souls. Not to mention the fact that nothing has been [divinely] commanded or enjoined upon us

concerning the dead. Therefore all this may be safely omitted, even if it were no error and idolatry.

13] The Papists quote here Augustine and some of the Fathers who are said to have written concerning purgatory,
and they think that we do not understand for what purpose
and to what end they spoke as they did. St. Augustine does
not write that there is a purgatory, nor has he a testimony
of Scripture to constrain him thereto, but he leaves it in
doubt whether there is one, and says that his mother asked
to be remembered at the altar or Sacrament. Now, all this is
indeed nothing but the devotion of men, and that, too, of
individuals, and does not establish an article of faith, which
is the prerogative of God alone.

14] Our Papists, however, cite such statements [opinions]
of men in order that men should believe in their horrible,
blasphemous, and cursed traffic in masses for souls in purgatory [or in sacrifices for the dead and oblations], etc. But
they will never prove these things from Augustine. Now,
when they have abolished the traffic in masses for purgatory, of which Augustine never dreamt, we will then discuss
with them whether the expressions of Augustine without
Scripture [being without the warrant of the Word] are to be
admitted, and whether the dead should be remembered at
the Eucharist. 15] For it will not do to frame articles of faith
from the works or words of the holy Fathers; otherwise
their kind of fare, of garments, of house, etc., would have
to become an article of faith, as was done with relics. [We
have, however, another rule, namely] The rule is: The Word
of God shall establish articles of faith, and no one else, not
even an angel.

16] Secondly. From this it has followed that evil spirits have
perpetrated much knavery [exercised their malice] by ap-
pearing as the souls of the departed, and with unspeakable

[horrible] lies and tricks demanded masses, vigils, pilgrimages, and other alms. 17] All of which we had to receive as articles of faith, and to live accordingly; and the Pope confirmed these things, as also the Mass and all other abominations. Here, too, there is no [cannot and must not be any] yielding or surrendering.

18] Thirdly. [Hence arose] the pilgrimages. Here, too, masses, the remission of sins and the grace of God were sought, for the Mass controlled everything. Now it is indeed certain that such pilgrimages, without the Word of God, have not been commanded us, neither are they necessary, since we can have these things [the soul can be cared for] in a better way, and can omit these pilgrimages without any sin and danger. Why therefore do they leave at home [desert] their own parish [their called ministers, their parishes], the Word of God, wives, children, etc., who are ordained and [attention to whom is necessary and has been] commanded, and run after these unnecessary, uncertain, pernicious will-o'-the-wisps of the devil [and errors]? 19] Unless the devil was riding [made insane] the Pope, causing him to praise and establish these practices, whereby the people again and again revolted from Christ to their own works, and became idolaters, which is worst of all; moreover, it is neither necessary nor commanded, but is senseless and doubtful, and besides harmful. Hence here, too, there can be no yielding or surrendering [to yield or concede anything here is not lawful], etc. 20] And let this be preached, that such pilgrimages are not necessary, but dangerous; and then see what will become of them. [For thus they will perish of their own accord.]

21] Fourthly. Fraternities [or societies], in which cloisters, chapters, vicars have assigned and communicated (by a legal contract and sale) all masses and good works, etc., both for the living and the dead. This is not only altogether a human bauble, without the Word of God, entirely unnecessary and not commanded, but also contrary to the chief article, Of Redemption. Therefore it is in no way to be tolerated.

22] Fifthly. The relics, in which there are found so many falsehoods and tomfooleries concerning the bones of dogs and horses, that even the devil has laughed at such rascalities, ought long ago to have been condemned, even though there were some good in them; and so much the more because they are without the Word of God; being neither commanded nor counseled, they are an entirely unnecessary and useless thing. 23] But the worst is that [they have imagined that] these relics had to work indulgence and the forgiveness of sins [and have revered them] as a good work and service of God, like the Mass, etc.

24] Sixthly. Here belong the precious indulgences granted (but only for money) both to the living and the dead, by which the miserable [sacrilegious and accursed] Judas, or Pope, has sold the merit of Christ, together with the superfluous merits of all saints and of the entire Church, etc. All these things [and every single one of them] are not to be borne, and are not only without the Word of God, without necessity, not commanded, but are against the chief article. For the merit of Christ is [apprehended and] obtained not by our works or pence, but from grace through faith, without money and merit; and is offered [and presented] not through the power of the Pope, but through the preaching of God's Word.

Of the Invocation of Saints.

25] The invocation of saints is also one of the abuses of Antichrist conflicting with the chief article, and destroys the

knowledge of Christ. Neither is it commanded nor counseled, nor has it any example [or testimony] in Scripture,
and even though it were a precious thing, as it is not [while,
on the contrary, it is a most harmful thing], in Christ we
have everything a thousandfold better [and surer, so that
we are not in need of calling upon the saints].

26] And although the angels in heaven pray for us (as
Christ Himself also does), as also do the saints on earth,
and perhaps also in heaven, yet it does not follow thence
that we should invoke and adore the angels and saints, and
fast, hold festivals, celebrate Mass in their honor, make of-
ferings, and establish churches, altars, divine worship, and
in still other ways serve them, and regard them as helpers
in need [as patrons and intercessors], and divide among
them all kinds of help, and ascribe to each one a particular
form of assistance, as the Papists teach and do. For this is
idolatry, and such honor belongs alone to God. 27] For as
a Christian and saint upon earth you can pray for me, not
only in one, but in many necessities. But for this reason I
am not obliged to adore and invoke you, and celebrate festivals, fast, make oblations, hold masses for your honor [and
worship], and put my faith in you for my salvation. I can in
other ways indeed honor, love, and thank you in Christ. 28]
If now such idolatrous honor were withdrawn from angels
and departed saints, the remaining honor would be without
harm and would quickly be forgotten. For when advantage
and assistance, both bodily and spiritual, are no more to
be expected, the saints will not be troubled [the worship
of the saints will soon vanish], neither in their graves nor
in heaven. For without a reward or out of pure love no one
will much remember, or esteem, or honor them [bestow on
them divine honor].

29] In short, the Mass itself and anything that proceeds from it, and anything that is attached to it, we cannot tolerate, but must condemn, in order that we may retain the holy Sacrament pure and certain, according to the institution of Christ, employed and received through faith.

Part II, Article III: Of Chapters and Cloisters.

1] That *chapters* and *cloisters* [colleges of canons and communistic dwellings], which were formerly founded with the good intention [of our forefathers] to educate learned men and chaste [and modest] women, ought again to be turned to such use, in order that pastors, preachers, and other ministers of the churches may be had, and likewise other necessary persons [fitted] for [the political administration of] the secular government [or for the commonwealth] in cities and countries, and well-educated, maidens for mothers and housekeepers, etc.

2] If they will not serve this purpose, it is better that they be abandoned or razed, rather than [continued and], with their blasphemous services invented by men, regarded as something better than the ordinary Christian life and the offices and callings ordained by God. For all this also is contrary to the first chief article concerning the redemption made through Jesus Christ. Add to this that (like all other human inventions) these have neither been commanded; they are needless and useless, and, besides, afford occasion for dangerous and vain labor [dangerous annoyances and fruitless worship], such services as the prophets call *Aven*, *i.e.*, pain and labor.

Part II, Article IV: Of the Papacy.

1] That *the Pope is not, according to divine law or according to the Word of God the head of all Christendom* (for this [name] belongs to One only, whose name is Jesus Christ), but is only the bishop and pastor of the Church at Rome, and of those who voluntarily or through a human creature (that is, a political magistrate) have attached themselves to him, to be Christians, not under him as a lord, but with him as brethren [colleagues] and comrades, as the ancient councils and the age of St. Cyprian show.

2] But to-day none of the bishops dare to address the Pope as brother as was done at that time [in the age of Cyprian]; but they must call him most gracious lord, even though they be kings or emperors. This [Such arrogance] we will not, cannot, must not take upon our conscience [with a good conscience approve]. Let him, however, who will do it, do so without us [at his own risk].

3] Hence it follows that all things which the Pope, from a power so false, mischievous, blasphemous, and arrogant, has done and undertaken, have been and still are purely diabolical affairs and transactions (with the exception of such things as pertain to the secular government, where God often permits much good to be effected for a people, even through a tyrant and [faithless] scoundrel) for the ruin of the entire holy [catholic or] Christian Church (so far as it is in his power) and for the destruction of the first and chief article concerning the redemption made through Jesus Christ.

4] For all his bulls and books are extant, in which he roars like a lion (as the angel in Rev. 12 depicts him, [crying out] that no Christian can be saved unless he obeys him and is subject to him in all things that he wishes, that he says, and that he does. All of which amounts to nothing less than saying: Although you believe in Christ, and have in Him [alone] everything that is necessary to salvation, yet it is nothing and all in vain unless you regard [have and worship] me as your god, and be subject and obedient to me. And yet it is manifest that the holy Church has been without the Pope for at least more than five hundred years, and that even to the present day the churches of the Greeks and of many other languages neither have been nor are yet under the Pope. 5] Besides, as often remarked, it is a human figment which is not commanded, and is unnecessary and useless; for the holy Christian [or catholic] Church can exist very well without such a head, and it would certainly have remained better [purer, and its career would have been more prosperous] if such a head had not been raised up by the devil. 6] And the Papacy is also of no use in the Church, because it exercises no Christian office; and therefore it is necessary for the Church to continue and to exist without the Pope.

7] And supposing that the Pope would yield this point, so as not to be supreme by divine right or from God's command, but that we must have [there must be elected] a [certain] head, to whom all the rest adhere [as their support] in order that the [concord and] unity of Christians may be preserved against sects and heretics, and that such a head were chosen by men, and that it were placed within the choice and power of men to change or remove this head, just as the Council of Constance adopted nearly this course with reference to the Popes, deposing three and electing a fourth; supposing, I say, that the Pope and See at Rome would yield and accept this (which, nevertheless, is impossible; for thus he would have to suffer his entire realm and estate to be overthrown and destroyed, with all his rights and books, a thing which, to speak in few words, he cannot do), nevertheless, even in this way Christianity would not be helped, but many more sects would arise than before.

8] For since men would have to be subject to this head, not from God's command, but from their personal good pleasure, it would easily and in a short time be despised, and at last retain no member; neither would it have to be forever confined to Rome or any other place, but it might be wherever and in whatever church God would grant a man fit for the [taking upon him such a great] office. Oh, the complicated and confused state of affairs [perplexity] that would result!

9] Therefore the Church can never be better governed and preserved than if we all live under one head, Christ, and all the bishops equal in office (although they be unequal in gifts), be diligently joined in unity of doctrine, faith, Sacraments, prayer, and works of love, etc., as St. Jerome writes that the priests at Alexandria together and in common governed the churches, as did also the apostles, and afterwards all bishops throughout all Christendom, until the Pope raised his head above all.

10] This teaching shows forcefully that the Pope is the very Antichrist, who has exalted himself above, and opposed himself against Christ because he will not permit Christians to be saved without his power, which, nevertheless, is nothing, and is neither ordained nor commanded by God. 11] This is, properly speaking to *exalt himself above all that is called God* as Paul says, 2 Thess. 2:4. Even the Turks or the Tartars, great enemies of Christians as they are, do not do this, but they allow whoever wishes to believe in Christ, and take bodily tribute and obedience from Christians.

12] The Pope, however, prohibits this faith, saying that to be saved a person must obey him. This we are unwilling to do, even though on this account we must die in God s name. 13] This all proceeds from the fact that the Pope has wished to be called the supreme head of the Christian Church by divine right. Accordingly he had to make himself equal and superior to Christ, and had to cause himself to be proclaimed the head and then the lord of the Church, and finally of the whole world, and simply God on earth, until he has dared to issue commands even to the angels in heaven. 14] And when we distinguish the Pope's teaching from, or measure and hold it against, Holy Scripture, it is found [it appears plainly] that the Pope's teaching, where it is best, has been taken from the imperial and heathen law, and treats of political matters and decisions or rights, as the Decretals show; furthermore, it teaches of ceremonies concerning churches, garments, food, persons and [similar] puerile, theatrical and comical things without measure, but in all these things nothing at all of Christ, faith, and the commandments of God. Lastly, it is nothing else than the devil himself, because above and against God he urges [and disseminates] his [papal] falsehoods concerning masses, purgatory, the monastic life, one's own works and [fictitious] divine worship (for this is the very Papacy [upon each of which the Papacy is altogether founded and is standing]), and condemns, murders and tortures all Christians who do not exalt and honor these abominations [of the Pope] above all things. Therefore, just as little as we can worship the devil himself as Lord and God, we can endure his apostle, the Pope, or Antichrist, in his rule as head or lord. For to lie and to kill, and to destroy body and soul eternally, that is wherein his papal government really consists, as I have very clearly shown in many books.

15] In these four articles they will have enough to condemn in the Council. For they cannot and will not concede us even the least point in one of these articles. Of this we should be certain, and animate ourselves with [be forewarned and made firm in] the hope that Christ, our Lord, has attacked His adversary, and he will press the attack home [pursue and destroy him] both by His Spirit and coming. Amen.

16] For in the Council we will stand not before the Emperor or the political magistrate, as at Augsburg (where the Emperor published a most gracious edict, and caused matters to be heard kindly [and dispassionately]), but [we will appear] before the Pope and devil himself, who intends to listen to nothing, but merely [when the case has been publicly announced] to condemn, to murder and to force us to idolatry. Therefore we ought not here to kiss his feet, or to say: "Thou art my gracious lord", but as the angel in Zechariah 3:2 said to Satan: *The Lord rebuke thee, O Satan.*

SA II Study Questions

1. Luther begins SA II in article I by distinguishing between the law and the gospel. Have you heard of this distinction before? What do you think about it? Is it important? Do you have a similar tool that guides your understanding of the faith?

2. Luther calls article I the article upon which everything stands. Is this article that important? What is the article upon which everything stands for you?

3. Luther uses article I as the basis of his offensive on articles II, III, and IV. In what way(s) did you see Luther doing this? Did he do a good job?

4. In the last paragraph of SA II Luther writes, "For in the Council we will stand not before the Emperor or the political magistrate, as at Augsburg (where the Emperor published a most gracious edict, and caused

matters to be heard kindly [and dispassionately]), but [we will appear] before the Pope and devil himself, who intends to listen to nothing, but merely [when the case has been publicly announced] to condemn, to murder and to force us to idolatry. Therefore we ought not here to kiss his feet, or to say: "Thou art my gracious lord", but as the angel in Zechariah 3:2 said to Satan: *The Lord rebuke thee, O Satan.*" How do you stand or witness to others when you know you have already been condemned? Does the faith you proclaim mean enough to you that you would stand trial at a rigged trial?

7

Smalcald Articles Section III

SA III Reflection

SA III begins the section Luther believed the reformers and the Roman church could come to some agreement on about the biblical truth. While writing this section, SA III, 4, Luther suffered an apparent heart attack. Thus from SA III, 4 "Concerning the Gospel" forward, Luther dictates the rest of the SA to Caspar Cruciger.[1] I include this fact as a reminder that for Luther, the idea of this being his last will and testament meant a lot. What is interesting about SA III is that it contains the most articles; in some ways it is also the most applicable to daily life.

For example, SA I, 1 deals with sin. How many times have you talked to someone about sin? What it is, and what it is not? Where it came from, and how it is dealt with? The amazing thing about sin is that even those who are not confessing Christians know about it and have opinions about

1. Kolb, "Smalcald Articles," 319 Note 127.

it. Another example can be found in SA II, 12, which deals with the church. Here is a topic that gets a lot of discussion time at Thanksgiving at our house. Are your kids going to church? Which church are they attending? A Presbyterian church? But they were raised Lutheran? What happened? Are you getting the point?

A few things to note as you read SA III. First, SA III, 4, "Concerning the Gospel," is the central article of SA III. If you read closely you might notice that articles I, II, and III all seem to lead up to the good news in article IV, and then article 4 indicates what is to come in the rest of SA III. Russell writes, "Article 4 itself also indicates what is to come in SA, Part III. Luther's list of the various ways in which the gospel becomes meaningful and relevant in human life forms the order of succeeding topics to be addressed in SA III, as Articles 5-8 clarify and explicate SA III, 4."[2] In other words, the disagreements in SA II about the doctrine of justification were not items that could be overcome. However, the gospel and its implication were items that reasonable people could come to a biblical understanding on. Thus, article IV in SA III is the key article in SA III because it gives life to all the other articles.

Second, and last, as you read SA III, notice that the gospel isn't so much defined; rather, SA III describes how the gospel becomes meaningful in everyday life. In other words, the gospel here is not an abstract topic for theologians' debate—it is where the "rubber meets the road." As you read this section, think about the "application" section of your own theological last will and testament. What would you include here? What are the topics your loved ones already debate? What are your opinions on those topics?

2. Russell, 96.

Smalcald Articles Section III Text

The Third Part of the Articles.

Concerning the following articles we may [will be able to] treat with learned and reasonable men, or among ourselves. The Pope and his [the Papal] government do not care much about these. For with them conscience is nothing, but money, [glory] honors, power are [to them] everything.

Part III, Article I. Of Sin

1] Here we must confess, as Paul says in Rom. 5:12, that sin originated [and entered the world] from one man Adam, by whose disobedience all men were made sinners, [and] subject to death and the devil. This is called original or capital sin.

2] The fruits of this sin are afterwards the evil deeds which are forbidden in the Ten Commandments, such as [distrust] unbelief, false faith, idolatry, to be without the fear of God, presumption [recklessness], despair, blindness [or complete *loss of sight*], and, in short not to know or regard God; furthermore to lie, to swear by [to abuse] God's name [to swear falsely], not to pray, not to call upon God, not to regard [to despise or neglect] God's Word, to be disobedient to parents, to murder, to be unchaste, to steal, to deceive, etc.

3] This hereditary sin is so deep [and horrible] a corruption of nature that no reason can understand it, but it must be [learned and] believed from the revelation of Scriptures, Ps. 51:5; Rom. 6:12ff; Ex. 33:3; Gen. 3:7ff Hence, it is nothing but error and blindness in regard to this article what the scholastic doctors have taught, namely:

4] *That since the fall of Adam the natural powers of man have remained entire and incorrupt, and that man by nature has a right reason and a good will; which things the philosophers teach.*

5] *Again, that man has a free will to do good and omit evil, and, conversely, to omit good and do evil.*

6] *Again, that man by his natural powers can observe and keep [do] all the commands of God.*

7] *Again, that, by his natural powers, man can love God above all things and his neighbor as himself.*

8] *Again, if a man does as much as is in him, God certainly grants him His grace.*

9] *Again, if he wishes to go to the Sacrament, there is no need of a good intention to do good, but it is sufficient if he has not a wicked purpose to commit sin; so entirely good is his nature and so efficacious the Sacrament.*

10] [Again,] *that it is not founded upon Scripture that for a good work the Holy Ghost with His grace is necessary.*

11] Such and many similar things have arisen from want of understanding and ignorance as regards both this sin and Christ, our Savior, and they are truly heathen dogmas, which we cannot endure. For if this teaching were right [approved], then Christ has died in vain, since there is in man no defect nor sin for which he should have died; or He would have died only for the body, not for the soul, inasmuch as the soul is [entirely] sound, and the body only is subject to death.

Part III, Article II. Of the Law

1] Here we hold that the Law was given by God, first, to restrain sin by threats and the dread of punishment, and by the promise and offer of grace and benefit. But all this miscarried on account of the wickedness which sin has wrought in man. 2] For thereby a part [some] were rendered worse, those, namely, who are hostile to [hate] the Law, because it forbids what they like to do, and enjoins what they do not like to do. Therefore, wherever they can escape [if they were not restrained by] punishment, they [would] do more against the Law than before. These, then, are the rude and wicked [unbridled and secure] men, who do evil wherever they [notice that they] have the opportunity.

3] The rest become blind and arrogant [are smitten with arrogance and blindness], and [insolently] conceive the opinion that they observe and can observe the Law by their own powers, as has been said above concerning the scholastic theologians; thence come the hypocrites and [self-righteous or] false saints.

4] But the chief office or force of the Law is that it reveal original sin with all its fruits, and show man how very low his nature has fallen, and has become [fundamentally and] utterly corrupted; as the Law must tell man that he has no God nor regards [cares for] God, and worships other gods, a matter which before and without the Law he would not have believed. In this way he becomes terrified, is humbled, desponds, despairs, and anxiously desires aid, but sees no escape; he begins to be an enemy of [enraged at] God, and to murmur, etc. 5] This is what Paul says, Rom. 4:15: *The Law worketh wrath.* And Rom. 5:20: *Sin is increased by the Law.* [*The Law entered that the offense might abound.*]

Part III, Article III. Of Repentance.

1] This office [of the Law] the New Testament retains and urges, as St. Paul, Rom. 1:18 does, saying: *The wrath of God is revealed from heaven against all ungodliness and unrighteousness of men.* Again, Rom 3:19: *All the world is guilty before God. No man is righteous before Him.* And Christ says, John 16:8: *The Holy Ghost will reprove the world of sin.*

2] This, then, is the thunderbolt of God by which He strikes in a heap [hurls to the ground] both manifest sinners and false saints [hypocrites], and suffers no one to be in the right [declares no one righteous], but drives them all together to terror and despair. This is the hammer, as Jeremiah 23:29 says: *Is not My Word like a hammer that breaketh the rock in pieces?* This is not *activa contritio* or manufactured repentance, but *passiva contritio* [torture of conscience], true sorrow of heart, suffering and sensation of death.

3] This, then, is what it means to begin true repentance; and here man must hear such a sentence as this: You are all of no account, whether you be manifest sinners or saints [in your own opinion]; you all must become different and do otherwise than you now are and are doing [no matter what sort of people you are], whether you are as great, wise, powerful, and holy as you may. Here no one is [righteous, holy], godly, etc.

4] But to this office the New Testament immediately adds the consolatory promise of grace through the Gospel, which must be believed, as Christ declares, Mark 1:15: *Repent and believe the Gospel, i.e.,* become different and do otherwise, and believe My promise. And John, preceding Him, is called a preacher of repentance, however, for the remission of sins, *i.e.,* John was to accuse all, and convict them of being sinners, that they might know what they were before God, and might acknowledge that they were lost men, and might thus be prepared for the Lord, to receive grace, and to expect and accept from Him the remission of sins. Thus also Christ Himself says, Luke 24:47: 6] *Repentance and remission of sins must be preached in My name among all nations.*

7] But whenever the Law alone, without the Gospel being added exercises this its office there is [nothing else than] death and hell, and man must despair, like Saul and Judas; as St. Paul, Rom. 7:10, says: *Through sin the Law killeth.* 8] On the other hand, the Gospel brings consolation and remission not only in one way, but through the word and Sacraments, and the like, as we shall hear afterward in order that [thus] there is *with the Lord plenteous redemption*, as Ps. 130:7 says against the dreadful captivity of sin.

9] However, we must now contrast the false repentance of the sophists with true repentance, in order that both may be the better understood.

Of the False Repentance of the Papists.

10] It was impossible that they should teach correctly concerning repentance, since they did not [rightly] know the real sins [the real sin]. For, as has been shown above, they do not believe aright concerning original sin, but say that the natural powers of man have remained [entirely] unimpaired and incorrupt; that reason can teach aright, and the will can in accordance therewith do aright [perform those things which are taught]; that God certainly bestows His grace when a man does as much as is in him, according to his free will.

11] It had to follow thence [from this dogma] that they did [must do] penance only for actual sins, such as wicked thoughts to which a person yields (for wicked emotion [concupiscence, vicious feelings, and inclinations], lust and improper dispositions [according to them] are not sins), and for wicked words and wicked deeds, which free will could readily have omitted.

12] And of such repentance they fix three parts, contrition, confession, and satisfaction, with this [magnificent] consolation and promise added: If man truly repent, [feel remorse,] confess, render satisfaction, he thereby would have merited forgiveness, and paid for his sins before God [atoned for his sins and obtained a plenary redemption]. Thus in repentance they instructed men to repose confidence in their own works. 13] Hence the expression originated, which was employed in the pulpit when public absolution was announced to the people: *Prolong O God, my life, until I shall make satisfaction for my sins and amend my life.*

14] There was here [profound silence and] no mention of Christ nor faith; but men hoped by their own works to overcome and blot out sins before God. And with this intention we became priests and monks, that we might array ourselves against sin.

15] As to contrition, this is the way it was done: Since no one could remember all his sins (especially as committed through an entire year), they inserted this provision, namely, that if an unknown sin should be remembered later [if the remembrance of a concealed sin should perhaps return], this also must be repented of and confessed, etc. Meanwhile they were [the person was] commended to the grace of God.

16] Moreover, since no one could know how great the contrition ought to be in order to be sufficient before God, they gave this consolation: He who could not have contrition, at least ought to have attrition, which I may call half a contrition or the beginning of contrition; for they have themselves understood neither of these terms nor do they understand them now, as little as I. Such attrition was reckoned as contrition when a person went to confession.

17] And when it happened that any one said that he could not have contrition nor lament his sins (as might have occurred in illicit love or the desire for revenge, etc.), they asked whether he did not wish or desire to have contrition [lament]. When one would reply Yes (for who, save the devil himself, would here say No?), they accepted this as contrition, and forgave him his sins on account of this good work of his [which they adorned with the name of contrition]. Here they cited the example of St. Bernard, etc.

18] Here we see how blind reason, in matters pertaining to God, gropes about, and, according to its own imagination, seeks for consolation in its own works, and cannot think of [entirely forgets] Christ and faith. But if it be [clearly] viewed in the light, this contrition is a manufactured and fictitious thought [or imagination], derived from man's own powers, without faith and without the knowledge of Christ. And in it the poor sinner, when he reflected upon his own lust and desire for revenge, would sometimes [perhaps] have laughed rather than wept [either laughed or wept, rather than to think of something else], except such as either had been truly struck by [the lightning of] the Law, or had been vainly vexed by the devil with a sorrowful spirit. Otherwise [with the exception of these persons] such contrition was certainly mere hypocrisy, and did not mortify the lust for sins [flames of sin]; for they had to grieve, while they would rather have continued to sin, if it had been free to them.

19] As regards confession, the procedure was this: Every one had [was enjoined] to enumerate all his sins (which is an impossible thing). This was a great torment. From such as he had forgotten [But if any one had forgotten some sins] he would be absolved on the condition that, if they would occur to him, he must still confess them. In this way he could never know whether he had made a sufficiently pure confession [perfectly and correctly], or when confessing would ever have an end. Yet he was pointed to his own works, and comforted thus: The more fully [sincerely and frankly] one confesses, and the more he humiliates himself and debases himself before the priest, the sooner and better he renders satisfaction for his sins; for such humility certainly would earn grace before God.

20] Here, too, there was no faith nor Christ, and the virtue of the absolution was not declared to him, but upon his enumeration of sins and his self-abasement depended his consolation. What torture, rascality, and idolatry such confession has produced is more than can be related.

21] As to satisfaction, this is by far the most involved [perplexing] part of all. For no man could know how much to render for a single sin, not to say how much for all. Here they have resorted to the device of imposing a small satisfaction, which could indeed be rendered, as five Paternosters, a day's fast, etc.; for the rest [that was lacking] of the [in their] repentance they were directed to purgatory.

22] Here, too, there was nothing but anguish and [extreme] misery. [For] some thought that they would never get out of purgatory, because, according to the old canons, seven years' repentance is required for a single mortal sin. 23] Nevertheless, confidence was placed upon our work of satisfaction, and if the satisfaction could have been perfect, confidence would have been placed in it entirely, and neither faith nor Christ would have been of use. But this confidence was impossible. For, although any one had done penance in that way for a hundred years, he would still not have known whether he had finished his penance. That meant forever to do penance and never to come to repentance.

24] Here now the Holy See at Rome, coming to the aid of the poor Church, invented indulgences, whereby it forgave and remitted [expiation or] satisfaction, first, for a single instance, for seven years, for a hundred years and distributed them among the cardinals and bishops, so that one could grant indulgence for a hundred years and another for a hundred days. But he reserved to himself alone the power to remit the entire satisfaction.

25] Now, since this began to yield money, and the traffic in bulls became profitable he devised the golden jubilee year [a truly gold-bearing year], and fixed it at Rome. He called this the remission of all punishment and guilt. Then the people came running, because every one would fain have been freed from this grievous, unbearable burden. This meant to find [dig up] and raise the treasures of the earth. Immediately the Pope pressed still further, and multiplied the golden years one upon another. But the more he devoured money, the wider grew his maw.

Later, therefore, he issued them [those golden years of his] by his legates [everywhere] to the countries, until all churches and houses were full of the Golden Year. 26] At last he also made an inroad into purgatory among the dead, first, by founding masses and vigils, afterwards, by indulgences and the Golden Year, and finally souls became so cheap that he released one for a farthing.

27] But all this, too, was of no avail. For although the Pope taught men to depend upon, and trust in, these indulgences [for salvation], yet he rendered the [whole] matter again uncertain. For in his bulls he declares: Whoever would share in the indulgences or a Golden Year must be contrite, and have confessed, and pay money. Now, we have heard above that this contrition and confession are with them uncertain and hypocrisy. Likewise, also no one knew what soul was in purgatory, and if some were therein, no one knew which had properly repented and confessed. Thus he took the precious money [the Pope snatched up the holy pence], and comforted them meanwhile with [led them to confidence in] his power and indulgence, and [then again led them away from that and] directed them again to their uncertain work.

28] If, now [although], there were some who did not believe [acknowledge] themselves guilty of such actual sins in [committed by] thoughts, words, and works,—as I, and such as I, in monasteries and chapters [fraternities or colleges of priests], wished to be monks and priests, and by fasting, watching, praying, saying Mass, coarse garments, and hard beds, etc., fought against [strove to resist] evil thoughts, and in full earnest and with force wanted to be holy, and yet the hereditary, inborn evil sometimes did in sleep what it is wont to do (as also St. Augustine and Jerome among others confess),—still each one held the other in esteem, so that some, according to our teaching, were regarded as holy, without sin and full of good works, so much so that with this mind we would communicate and sell our good works to others, as being superfluous to us for heaven. This is indeed true, and seals, letters, and instances [that this happened] are at hand.

29] [When there were such, I say,] These did not need repentance. For of what would they repent, since they had not indulged wicked thoughts? What would they confess [concerning words not uttered], since they had avoided words? For what should they render satisfaction, since they were so guiltless of any deed that they could even sell their superfluous righteousness to other poor sinners? Such saints were also the Pharisees and scribes in the time of Christ.

30] Here comes the fiery angel, St. John [Rev. 10], the true preacher of [true] repentance, and with one [thunderclap and] bolt hurls both [those selling and those buying works] on one heap, and says: *Repent*! Matt. 3:2. 31] Now, the former [the poor wretches] imagine: Why, we have repented! The latter [the rest] say: We need no repentance. 32] John says: Repent ye, both of you, for ye are false penitents; so are these [the rest] false saints [or hypocrites], and all of you on either side need the forgiveness of sins, because neither of you know what true sin is not to say anything about your duty to repent of it and shun it. For no one of you is good; you are full of unbelief, stupidity, and ignorance of God and God's will. For here He is present *of whose fulness have all we received, and grace for grace,* John 1:16, and without Him no man can be just before God. Therefore, if you wish to repent, repent aright; your penance will not accomplish anything [is nothing]. And you hypocrites, who do not need repentance, you serpents' brood, who has assured you that you will escape the wrath to come? etc. Matt. 3:7; Luke 3:7.

33] In the same way Paul also preaches, Rom. 3:10-12: *There is none righteous, there is none that understandeth, there is none that seeketh after God, there is none that doeth good, no not one; they are all gone out of the way; they are together become unprofitable.* 34] And Acts 17:30: *God now commandeth all men everywhere to repent.* "All men," he says; no one excepted who is a man. 35] This repentance teaches us to discern sin, namely, that we are altogether lost, and that there is nothing good in us from head to foot [both within and without], and that we must absolutely become new and other men.

36] This repentance is not piecemeal [partial] and beggarly [fragmentary], like that which does penance for actual sins, nor is it uncertain like that. For it does not debate what is or is not sin, but hurls everything on a heap, and says: All in us is nothing but sin [affirms that, with respect to us, all is simply sin (and there is nothing in us that is not sin and guilt)]. What is the use of [For why do we wish] investigating, dividing, or distinguishing a long time? For this reason, too, this contrition is not [doubtful or] uncertain. For there is nothing left with which we can think of any good thing to pay for sin, but there is only a sure despairing concerning all that we are, think, speak, or do [all hope must be cast aside in respect of everything], etc.

37] In like manner confession, too, cannot be false, uncertain, or piecemeal [mutilated or fragmentary]. For he who confesses that all in him is nothing but sin comprehends all sins, excludes none, forgets none. 38] Neither can the satisfaction be uncertain, because it is not our uncertain, sinful work, but it is the suffering and blood of the [spotless and] innocent Lamb of God who taketh away the sin of the world.

39] Of this repentance John preaches, and afterwards Christ in the Gospel, and we also. By this [preaching of] repentance we dash to the ground the Pope and everything that is built upon our good works. For all is built upon a rotten and vain foundation, which is called a good work or law, even though no good work is there, but only wicked works, and no one does the Law (as Christ, John 7:19, says), but all transgress it. Therefore the building [that is raised upon it] is nothing but falsehood and hypocrisy, even [in the part] where it is most holy and beautiful.

40] And in Christians this repentance continues until death, because, through the entire life it contends with sin remaining in the flesh, as Paul, Rom. 7:14-25, [shows] testifies that he *wars with the law in his members*, etc.; and that, not by his own powers, but by the gift of the Holy Ghost that follows the remission of sins. This gift daily cleanses and sweeps out the remaining sins, and works so as to render man truly pure and holy.

41] The Pope, the theologians, the jurists, and every other man know nothing of this [from their own reason], but it is a doctrine from heaven, revealed through the Gospel, and must suffer to be called heresy by the godless saints [or hypocrites].

42] On the other hand, if certain sectarists would arise, some of whom are perhaps already extant, and in the time of the insurrection [of the peasants] came to my own view, holding that all those who had once received the Spirit or the forgiveness of sins, or had become believers, even though they should afterwards sin, would still remain in the faith, and such sin would not harm them, and [hence] crying thus: "Do whatever you please; if you believe, it all amounts to nothing; faith blots out all sins," etc.—they say, besides, that if any one sins after he has received faith and the Spirit, he never truly had the Spirit and faith: I have had before me [seen and heard] many such insane men, and I fear that in some such a devil is still remaining [hiding and dwelling].

43] It is, accordingly, necessary to know and to teach that when holy men, still having and feeling original sin, also daily repenting of and striving with it, happen to fall into manifest sins, as David into adultery, murder, and blasphemy, that then faith and the Holy Ghost has departed from them [they cast out faith and the Holy Ghost]. For the Holy Ghost does not permit sin to have dominion, to gain the upper hand so as to be accomplished, but represses and restrains it so that it must not do what it wishes. But if it does what it wishes, the Holy Ghost and faith are [certainly] not present. For St. John says, 1 John 3:9: *Whosoever is born of God doth not commit sin . . . and he cannot sin.* And yet it is also the truth when the same St. John says, 1:8: *If we say that we have no sin, we deceive ourselves and the truth is not in us.*

Part III, Article IV. Of the Gospel.

We will now return to the Gospel, which not merely in one way gives us counsel and aid against sin; for God is superabundantly rich [and liberal] in His grace [and goodness]. First, through the spoken Word by which the forgiveness of sins is preached [He commands to be preached] in the whole world; which is the peculiar office of the Gospel. Secondly, through Baptism. Thirdly, through the holy Sacrament of the Altar. Fourthly, through the power of the keys, and also through the mutual conversation and consolation of brethren, Matt. 18:20: *Where two or three are gathered together*, etc.

Part III, Article V. Of Baptism.

1] Baptism is nothing else than the Word of God in the water, commanded by His institution, or, as Paul says, *a washing in the Word*; as also Augustine says: *Let the Word come to the element, and it becomes a Sacrament.* 2] And for this reason we do not hold with Thomas and the monastic preachers [or Dominicans] who forget the Word (God's institution) and say that God has imparted to the water a spiritual power, which through the water washes away sin. 3] Nor [do we agree] with Scotus and the Barefooted monks [Minorites or Franciscan monks], who teach that, by the assistance of the divine will, Baptism washes away sins, and that this ablution occurs only through the will of God, and by no means through the Word or water.

4] Of the baptism of children we hold that children ought to be baptized. For they belong to the promised redemption made through Christ, and the Church should administer it [Baptism and the announcement of that promise] to them.

Part III, Article VI. Of the Sacrament of the Altar.

1] Of the Sacrament of the Altar we hold that bread and wine in the Supper are the true body and blood of Christ, and are given and received not only by the godly, but also by wicked Christians.

2] And that not only one form is to be given. [For] we do not need that high art [specious wisdom] which is to teach us that under the one form there is as much as under both, as the sophists and the Council of Constance teach. 3] For even if it were true that there is as much under one as under both, yet the one form only is not the entire ordinance and institution [made] ordained and commanded by Christ. 4] And we especially condemn and in God's name execrate those who not only omit both forms but also quite autocratically [tyrannically] prohibit, condemn, and blaspheme them as heresy, and so exalt themselves against and above Christ, our Lord and God [opposing and placing themselves ahead of Christ], etc.

5] As regards transubstantiation, we care nothing about the sophistical subtlety by which they teach that bread and wine leave or lose their own natural substance, and that there remain only the appearance and color of bread, and not true bread. For it is in perfect agreement with Holy Scriptures that there is, and remains, bread, as Paul himself calls it, 1 Cor. 10:16: *The bread which we break.* And 1 Cor. 11:28: *Let him so eat of that bread.*

Part III, Article VII. Of the Keys.

1] The keys are an office and power given by Christ to the Church for binding and loosing sin, not only the gross and well-known sins, but also the subtle, hidden, which are known only to God, as it is written in Ps. 19:13: *Who can understand his errors?* And in Rom. 7:25 St. Paul himself complains *that with the flesh he serves the law of sin.* 2] For it is not in our power, but belongs to God alone, to judge which, how great, and how many the sins are, as it is written in Ps. 143:2: *Enter not into judgment with Thy servant; for in Thy sight shall no man living be justified.* 3] And Paul says, 1 Cor. 4:4: *For I know nothing by myself; yet am I not hereby justified.*

Part III, Article VIII. Of Confession.

1] Since Absolution or the Power of the Keys is also an aid and consolation against sin and a bad conscience, ordained by Christ [Himself] in the Gospel, Confession or Absolution ought by no means to be abolished in the Church, especially on account of [tender and] timid consciences and on account of the untrained [and capricious] young people, in order that they may be examined, and instructed in the Christian doctrine.

2] But the enumeration of sins ought to be free to every one, as to what he wishes to enumerate or not to enumerate. For as long as we are in the flesh, we shall not lie when we say: "I am a poor man [I acknowledge that I am a miserable sinner], full of sin." Rom. 7:23: *I see another law in my members*, etc. For since private absolution originates in the Office of the Keys, it should not be despised [neglected], but greatly and highly esteemed [of the greatest worth], as [also] all other offices of the Christian Church.

3] And in those things which concern the spoken, outward Word, we must firmly hold that God grants His Spirit or grace to no one, except through or with the preceding outward Word, in order that we may [thus] be protected against the enthusiasts, *i.e.*, spirits who boast that they have the Spirit without and before the Word, and accordingly judge Scripture or the spoken Word, and explain and stretch it at their pleasure, as Muenzer did, and many still do at the present day, who wish to be acute judges between the Spirit and the letter, and yet know not what they say or declare. 4] For [indeed] the Papacy also is nothing but sheer enthusiasm, by which the Pope boasts that all rights exist in the shrine of his heart, and whatever he decides and commands with [in] his church is spirit and right, even though it is above and contrary to Scripture and the spoken Word.

5] All this is the old devil and old serpent, who also converted Adam and Eve into enthusiasts, and led them from the outward Word of God to spiritualizing and self-conceit, and nevertheless he accomplished this through other outward words. 6] Just as also our enthusiasts [at the present day] condemn the outward Word, and nevertheless they themselves are not silent, but they fill the world with their pratings and writings, as though, indeed, the Spirit could not come through the writings and spoken word of the apostles, but [first] through their writings and words he must come. Why [then] do not they also omit their own sermons and writings, until the Spirit Himself come to men, without their writings and before them, as they boast that He has come into them without the preaching of the Scriptures? But of these matters there is not time now to dispute at greater length; we have elsewhere sufficiently urged this subject.

7] For even those who believe before Baptism, or become believing in Baptism, believe through the preceding out-ward Word, as the adults, who have come to reason, must first have heard: *He that believeth and is baptized shall be saved*, even though they are at first unbelieving, and receive the Spirit and Baptism ten years afterwards. 8] Cornelius, Acts 10:1ff , had heard long before among the Jews of the coming Messiah, through whom he was righteous before God, and in such faith his prayers and alms were acceptable to God (as Luke calls him devout and God-fearing), and without such preceding Word and hearing could not have believed or been righteous. But St. Peter had to reveal to him that the Messiah (in whom, as one that was to come, he had hitherto believed) now had come, lest his faith con-cerning the coming Messiah hold him captive among the hardened and unbelieving Jews, but know that he was now to be saved by the present Messiah, and must not, with the [rabble of the] Jews deny nor persecute Him.

9] In a word, enthusiasm inheres in Adam and his chil-dren from the beginning [from the first fall] to the end of the world, [its poison] having been implanted and infused into them by the old dragon, and is the origin, power [life], and strength of all heresy, especially of that of the Papacy and Mahomet. 10] Therefore we ought and must constantly maintain this point, that God does not wish to deal with us otherwise than through the spoken Word and the Sacraments. 11] It is the devil himself whatsoever is extolled as Spirit without the Word and Sacraments. For God wished to appear even to Moses through the burning bush and spoken Word; and no prophet neither Elijah nor Elisha, received the Spirit without the Ten Commandments [or spoken Word]. 12] Neither was John the Baptist conceived without the preceding word of Gabriel, nor did he leap in his mother's womb without the voice of Mary. 13] And Peter says, 2 Pet. 1:21: *The prophecy came not by the will of man; but holy men of God spake as they were moved by the Holy Ghost.* Without the outward Word, however, they were not holy, much less would the Holy Ghost have moved them to speak when they still were unholy [or profane]; for they were holy, says he, since the Holy Ghost spake through them.

Part III, Article IX. Of Excommunication.

The greater excommunication, as the Pope calls it, we regard only as a civil penalty, and it does not concern us ministers of the Church. But the lesser, that is, the true Christian excommunication, consists in this, that manifest and obstinate sinners are not admitted to the Sacrament and other communion of the Church until they amend their lives and avoid sin. And ministers ought not to mingle secular punishments with this ecclesiastical punishment, or excommunication.

Part III, Article X. Of Ordination and the Call.

1] If the bishops would be true bishops [would rightly discharge their office], and would devote themselves to the Church and the Gospel, it might be granted to them for the sake of love and unity, but not from necessity, to ordain and confirm us and our preachers; omitting, however, all comedies and spectacular display [deceptions, absurdities, and appearances] of unchristian [heathenish] parade and pomp. 2] But because they neither are, nor wish to be, true bishops, but worldly lords and princes, who will neither preach, nor teach, nor baptize, nor administer the Lord's Supper, nor perform any work or office of the Church, and, moreover, persecute and condemn those who discharge these functions, having been called to do so, the Church ought not on their account to remain without ministers [to be forsaken by or deprived of ministers].

3] Therefore, as the ancient examples of the Church and the Fathers teach us, we ourselves will and ought to ordain suitable persons to this office; and, even according to their own laws, they have not the right to forbid or prevent us. For their laws say that those ordained even by heretics should be declared [truly] ordained and stay ordained [and that such ordination must not be changed], as St. Jerome writes of the Church at Alexandria, that at first it was governed in common by priests and preachers, without bishops.

Part III, Article XI. Of the Marriage of Priests.

1] To prohibit marriage, and to burden the divine order of priests with perpetual celibacy, they have had neither authority nor right [they have done out of malice, without any honest reason], but have acted like antichristian, tyrannical, desperate scoundrels [have performed the work of antichrist, of tyrants and the worst knaves], and have thereby caused all kinds of horrible, abominable, innumerable sins of unchastity [depraved lusts], in which they still wallow. 2] Now, as little as we or they have been given the power to make a woman out of a man or a man out of a woman, or to nullify either sex, so little have they had the power to [sunder and] separate such creatures of God, or to forbid them from living [and cohabiting] honestly in marriage with one another. 3] Therefore we are unwilling to assent to their abominable celibacy, nor will we [even] tolerate it, but we wish to have marriage free as God has instituted [and ordained] it, and we wish neither to rescind nor hinder His work; for Paul says, 1 Tim. 4:1ff , that this [prohibition of marriage] is *a doctrine of devils.*

Part III, Article XII. Of the Church.

1] We do not concede to them that they are the Church, and [in truth] they are not [the Church]; nor will we listen to those things which, under the name of Church, they enjoin or forbid. 2] For, thank God, [to-day] a child seven years old knows what the Church is, namely, the holy believers and lambs who hear the voice of their Shepherd. For the children pray thus: *I believe in one holy* [catholic or] *Christian Church.* 3] This holiness does not consist in albs, tonsures, long gowns, and other of their ceremonies devised by them beyond Holy Scripture, but in the Word of God and true faith.

Part III, Article XIII. How One is Justified before God, and of Good Works.

1] What I have hitherto and constantly taught concerning this I know not how to change in the least, namely, that by faith, as St. Peter says, we acquire a new and clean heart, and God will and does account us entirely righteous and holy for the sake of Christ, our Mediator. And although sin in the flesh has not yet been altogether removed or become dead, yet He will not punish or remember it.

2] And such faith, renewal, and forgiveness of sins is followed by good works. And what there is still sinful or imperfect also in them shall not be accounted as sin or defect, even [and that, too] for Christ's sake; but the entire man, both as to his person and his works, is to be called and to be righteous and holy from pure grace and mercy, shed upon us [unfolded] and spread over us in Christ. 3] Therefore we cannot boast of many merits and works, if they are viewed apart from grace and mercy, but as it is written, 1 Cor. 1:31: *He that glorieth, let him glory in the Lord*, namely, that he has a gracious God. For thus all is well. 4] We say, besides, that if good works do not follow, faith is false and not true.

Part III, Article XIV. Of Monastic Vows.

1] As monastic vows directly conflict with the first chief article, they must be absolutely abolished. For it is of them that Christ says, Matt. 24:5, 23ff : *I am Christ*, etc. 2] For he who makes a vow to live as a monk believes that he will enter upon a mode of life holier than ordinary Christians lead, and wishes to earn heaven by his own works not only for himself, but also for others; this is to deny Christ. 3] And they boast from their St. Thomas that a monastic vow is equal to Baptism. This is blasphemy [against God].

Part III, Article XV. Of Human Traditions.

1] The declaration of the Papists that human traditions serve for the remission of sins, or merit salvation, is [altogether] unchristian and condemned, as Christ says Matt. 15:9: *In vain they do worship Me, teaching for doctrines the commandments of men.* 2] Again, Titus 1:14: *That turn from the truth.* Again, when they declare that it is a mortal sin if one breaks these ordinances [does not keep these statutes], this, too, is not right.

3] These are the articles on which I must stand, and, God willing, shall stand even to my death; and I do not know how to change or to yield anything in them. If any one wishes to yield anything, let him do it at the peril of his conscience.

4] Lastly, there still remains the Pope's bag of impostures concerning foolish and childish articles, as, the dedication of churches, the baptism of bells, the baptism of the altarstone, and the inviting of sponsors to these rites, who would make donations towards them. Such baptizing is a reproach and mockery of Holy Baptism, hence should not be tolerated. 5] Furthermore, concerning the consecration of wax-tapers, palm-branches, cakes, oats, [herbs,] spices, etc., which indeed, cannot be called consecrations, but are sheer mockery and fraud. And such deceptions there are without number, which we commend for adoration to their god and to themselves, until they weary of it. We will [ought to] have nothing to do with them.

1] *Dr. Martin Luther* subscribed.

2] *Dr. Justus Jonas*, Rector, subscribed with his own hand.

3] *Dr. John Bugenhagen, Pomeranus*, subscribed.

4] *Dr. Caspar Creutziger* subscribed.

5] *Niclas Ambsdorf* of Magdeburg subscribed.

6] *George Spalatin* of Altenburg subscribed.

7] I, *Philip Melanchthon*, also regard [approve] the above articles as right and Christian. But regarding the Pope I hold that, if he would allow the Gospel, his superiority over the bishops which he has otherwise, is conceded to him by human right also by us, for the sake of peace and general unity of those Christians who are also under him, and may be under him hereafter.

8] *John Agricola* of Eisleben subscribed.

9] *Gabriel Didymus* subscribed.

10] I, *Dr. Urban Rhegius*, Superintendent of the churches in the Duchy of Lueneburg, subscribe in my own name and in the name of my brethren, and of the Church of Hannover.

11] I, *Stephen Agricola*, Minister at Hof, subscribe.

12] Also I, *John Draconites*, Professor and Minister at Marburg, subscribe.

13] I, *Conrad Figenbotz*, for the glory of God subscribe that I have thus believed, and am still preaching and firmly believing as above.

14] I, *Andrew Osiander* of Nuernberg, subscribe.

15] I, Magister *Veit Dieterich*, Minister at Nuernberg, subscribe.

16] I, *Erhard Schnepf*, Preacher at Stuttgart, subscribe.

17] *Conrad Oetinger*, Preacher of Duke Ulrich at Pforzheim.

18] *Simon Schnevveis*, Pastor of the Church at Crailsheim.

19] I, *John Schlainhauffen*, Pastor of the Church at Koethen, subscribe.

20] The Reverend Magister *George Helt* of Forchheim.

21] The Reverend Magister *Adam of Fulda*, Preacher in Hesse.

22] The Reverend Magister *Anthony Corvinus*, Preacher in Hesse.

23] I, Doctor *John Bugenhagen, Pomeranus*, again subscribe in the name of Magister *John Brentz*, as on departing from Smalcald he directed me orally and by a letter, which I have shown to those brethren who have subscribed.

24] I, *Dionysius Melander*, subscribe to the Confession, the Apology, and the Concordia on the subject of the Eucharist.

25] *Paul Rhodius*, Superintendent of Stettin.

26] *Gerard Oeniken*, Superintendent of the Church at Minden.

27] I, *Brixius Northanus*, Minister of the Church of Christ which is at Soest, subscribe to the Articles of the Reverend Father Martin Luther, and confess that hitherto I have thus believed and taught, and by the Spirit of Christ I shall continue thus to believe and teach.

28] *Michael Coelius*, Preacher at Mansfeld, subscribed.

29] The Reverend Magister *Peter Geltner*, Preacher at Frankfort, subscribed.

30] *Wendal Faber*, Pastor of Seeburg in Mansfeld.

31] I, *John Aepinus*, subscribe.

32] Likewise, I, *John Amsterdam* of Bremen.

33] I, *Frederick Myconius*, Pastor of the Church at Gotha in Thuringia, subscribe in my own name and in that of *Justus Menius* of Eisenach.

34] I, Doctor *John Lang*, Preacher of the Church at Erfurt, subscribe with my own hand in my own name, and in that of my other coworkers in the Gospel, namely:

35] The Reverend Licentiate *Ludwig Platz* of Melsungen.

36] The Reverend Magister *Sigismund Kirchner*.

37] The Reverend *Wolfgang Kismetter*.

38] The Reverend *Melchior Weitmann*.

39] The Reverend *John Tall*.

40] The Reverend *John Kilian*.

41] The Reverend *Nicholas Faber*.

42] The Reverend *Andrew Menser*.

43] And I, *Egidius Mechler*, have subscribed with my own hand.

SA III Study Questions

1. Article IV, "Concerning the Gospel," is the heart of SA III. How is the gospel meaningful in your everyday life?

2. How will you craft your theological last will and testament to reflect how the gospel is meaningful in your everyday life?

3. When I think about laws I think about restrictions that, if broken, lead to punishment. Article II here concerns law, but its purpose seems to lead to Christ. How would you talk about sin and law in your theological last will and testament?

4. What do you think about all the articles in SA III? Are they important items still? What would your set look like?

8

What Now?

SO YOU HAVE NOW read, studied, and digested one of the more obscure confessional documents. What now? In the preface, I suggested that the SA speak more clearly to us today than the other documents. With this in mind, I now challenge you to take a shot and write your own theological last will and testament.

Why? Well, it's simple. In writing your own theological last will and testament, you will find that you actually redefine your own theological point of view. No longer will you allow others speak for you, but you will take ownership of your confession. Furthermore, writing your own theological last will and testament is an act of confession in and of itself, and this is part of what it means to be a Christian and a Lutheran. Robert Kolb, in his book *Confessing the Faith: Reformers Define the Church 1530-1580,* writes,

> Confessing the faith is simply a part of following Christ and a vital part of the Christian life. It has taken on particular significance in the Lutheran church because of the way in which Lutherans

> conceive of their callings and believers, and be-
> cause of the historic circumstances in which our
> confession were born.[1]

Luther and the reformers had to show that their understanding of justification was in line with scripture. In doing
so they confessed their faith, and we still do this today—although not as much as we should.

In a world driven by financial success and a need
to excel we are constantly confessing something, but the
question we need to be asking is whether or not what we
are confessing is Christ. As a father myself, I hope to pass
down many values to my children: hard work, open mind-
edness, a heart for serving those in need. However, more
than anything, what I hope to pass down to my children is
the knowledge of God in Christ, because this is the knowledge one can call upon in a time of need. It's the kind of
knowledge that sustains a person when the world makes no
sense, and it's the knowledge that brings a deep and abid-
ing comfort for a soul that has been broken. As you begin
to think about your theological last will and testament, I
encourage you to think about it in the same way you think
about passing down certain values to your children and
grandchildren, or to kids in general.

In an effort to encourage you to write your theological
last will and testament, allow me to suggest that you follow
the same format as Luther. Begin with a section on the faith
you inherited. What have you received from your tradition?
Then move onto a section of those things which you feel
biblically cannot be compromised. For Luther, this section
revolved around the doctrine of justification. Maybe for
you it will be the same, or maybe it will be a different belief
or doctrine. Then move on to a section that spells out the

1. Robert Kolb, *Confessing the Faith: Reformers Define the
Church, 1530-1580* (St. Louis: Concordia Publishing House, 1991), 9.

implications of your faith. Finally, I suggest you add a section that Luther did not: include a letter to your loved ones acknowledging why your faith is important to you and your hopes for their faith. Appendix A serves as a visual to guide you in your endeavor.

At a time when it seems as if there are fewer and fewer people in the pews, and when it appears as though people don't care anymore about their faith, a project like this will show your loved ones that your faith isn't just about checking off another requirement off the list to become a better person. Faith is about God engaging us. It's not something you have, it's something that is given to you so that in the midst of a broken world all might see the power of Christ's death and resurrection. When Jesus sent the disciples in Matthew 28 he said, "Go!" He didn't say, "Take what I have given you and keep it to yourself, so no one knows about it." He said, "Go! Make disciples, baptize and teach them!" It's now your turn to go and do as you were commanded. Proclaim the faith!

Your Theological Last Will and Testament Outline

Write down 3 tenets of the faith you received growing up:

1)

2)

3)

Write down 3 tenets of the faith that cannot be compromised, and explain why:

1)

2)

3)

Your Theological Last Will and Testament Outline

Write down 3 ways in which your faith influences how you live:

1)

2)

3)

Write a letter to your loved ones about why your faith is important, and what you hope for their faith lives:

Reformation Day Sermon

Reformation Sunday 2011

Romans 3:19-28

"For we hold that a person is justified by faith apart from works of the law."

Romans 3:28

In the name of the Father, and of the Son, and of the Holy Spirit, Amen.

Each and every year on Reformation Sunday we find ourselves recalling the story of Martin Luther nailing his 95 Theses to the Castle Church of Wittenberg. For us Lutherans in this room, it's kind nostalgic to recall this story not only because we love to tell it, but also because it reminds us of our beginnings. I don't want to retell this story today, though. Instead I want to tell you a different story. I want to tell you about the story of Luther's *Smalcald Articles*. While this story is not as well known, it should be, for it's the story of Luther's theological last will and testament.

This story begins in 1518, a year after Luther took to remodeling the church door in Wittenberg, and it begins with him calling for a general council in the church. You see, Luther realized that the Church had some issues, and rather than sit around and debate these issues, which Luther had been doing, he wanted to see change. Now I have to tell you Luther's call for a council took a while to be heard. As a matter of fact, Luther would wait nine years before his call was even acknowledged! Can you imagine that? I have a hard time waiting a week for something, much less years. And even after his call for a council was acknowledged, it wouldn't be until 1536 that the Pope would call for a council to meet in 1537. So after 19 years, a date would finally be set.

To prepare for this council, Luther was asked to write a little document which we know as the *Smalcald Articles*. Luther crafted these articles in such a way that they would allow future generations to have an authentic expression of the evangelical faith. In other words, the idea behind them was to provide a blueprint for what the reformers believed, taught, and confessed.

Now why am I telling you this? Why is this story important? Today we read in Paul's letter to the Romans, "We hold a person is justified by faith apart from works of the law." In this theological last will and testament, Luther writes, "In this article nothing can be given up or compromised." And he goes on to write, "On this article rests all we teach and practice." This is the heart of the Reformation. This is what Luther wanted to pass on to future generations, because this is the heart of the biblical message!

As we gather today in response to God's gracious act of mercy and love, and as we celebrate and remember the Reformation, we do so not because Luther nailed paper to a door. There is nothing special or amazing about what Luther did to that church door. No, today we gather to celebrate the heart of the Gospel's message: Jesus Christ died for you. No more clearly is this proclaimed than in Paul's letter to the Romans.

But let me ask you: While we know that we are justified by faith and not by works, do we understand the words we hear in our reading? Law, faith, righteousness of God? There is a difference between knowing and understanding. I know my mom loves me, but some days I don't understand why. We know we are justified by faith, but do we understand what this means?

Paul writes this letter to the Romans, who already know something about Jesus and why he was important. So in writing to a church that knows Jesus, Paul writes to clarify what they know and bring them to a deeper understanding. To do this he starts with the basics. In Chapter one, Paul says the gospel is the power of God for salvation to all who have faith, and this has been revealed to all. In Chapter two, Paul says that because it has been revealed to all no one has an excuse not to understand it, yet because there is a lack of understanding it is evident that all have fallen short of God's righteousness. In Chapter three Paul is led to declare that no one is righteous. And this is where we pick up today. No one is righteous before God; indeed, all have fallen short.

So our question leading up to today was this: How is one made righteous? If all have fallen short of God's expectations, how is a person justified before God? Paul says, "No human being will be justified in his sight by deeds prescribed by the law, for through the law comes the knowledge of sin." So what we need to realize here is that Paul, up to this point, has been setting us up. The Law does three things. It orders society by providing us law that keep us safe. It teaches us how to live in God-pleasing ways. Finally, and most importantly, it exposes our sin.

Let me illustrate this with a story. Right before my wife and I were married, I was traveling from Ephrata, Washington to Tacoma, Washington. As I got off I-90 and got on Highway 18 I kept driving what I thought was the speed limit: 70 mph. After a few minutes of driving I was pulled over by a police officer who informed me that the speed limit was actually 60 mph. Now I didn't know I was breaking the law until the police officer told me. This is exactly what Paul is doing today. The law shows how we have transgressed and points us to what saves us: Christ. In other words, when understood correctly, the law points us to Christ, who makes us new.

But Paul goes on. He says the righteousness of God is manifested apart from the law. Remember, the righteousness of God terrified Luther. This righteousness led Luther to think that God was only an angry judge who sought vengeance. This image was hard on Luther because he struggled to love a God who was so angry. However, Luther eventually came to realize that God's righteousness isn't found in his judgment, but it is found in Christ. This was a breakthrough moment for him. God's goodness isn't found in a person's ability to appease God. It's found in Christ!

The law tells us that we need Christ, and God's righteousness is a gift that comes through faith. So what does it mean to be justified by faith? It means that we are all sinners, and we have all fallen short of God's glory. If we were not sinners, then we wouldn't need to be here. Yet because we are sinners, we also have promised to us Christ, who comes and takes away our sins!

The *Smalcald Articles* called this the article upon which the church stood or fell. The church stands and falls on this article because we stand or fall on God's goodness and grace. In his last theological will and testament, Luther said this could never be compromised. Why? It's simple: To compromise this article is to compromise the comfort that only Christ brings. As we celebrate the Reformation today, we gather to celebrate the faith that has been passed down to us from our ancestors and the faith that we will pass down to our children. The heart of that faith is simple: "A person is justified by faith." As you leave this place and go out into the world, where you will be shown the many ways in which you don't live up to what is expected, hold tight to this message. You are justified, you are made right, you are reconciled with God not because of what you have done, but only because of what Christ has done for you.

Amen.

Bibliography

Arand, Charles P., Robert Kolb, and James A. Nestingen. *The Lutheran Confessions: History and Theology of The Book of Concord.* Minneapolis: Fortress Press, 2012.

Bente, F., and W.H.T. Dau, trans. *Triglot Concordia: The Symbolical Books of the Evangelical Lutheran Church: German-Latin-English.* Saint Louis, Missouri: Concordia Publishing House, 1921. Retrieved from http://bookofconcord.org/index.php

Edwards, Jr. Mark U., *Luther's Last Battles: Politics and Polemics 1531–46.* Ithaca, New York: Cornell University Press, 1983.

Kolb, Robert. *Confessing the Faith: Reformers Define the Church, 1530–1580.* St. Louis: Concordia Publishing House, 1991.

Kolb, Robert, and Timothy J. Wengert, eds. The Book of Concord: *The Confessions of the Evangelical Lutheran Church.* Translated by Charles Arand, Eric Gritsch, Robert Kolb, William Russell, James Schaaf, Jane Strohl, and Timothy J. Wengert. Minneapolis, Minnesota: Fortress Press, 2000.

Lull, Timothy F., ed. *Martin Luther's Basic Theological Writings.* 2nd ed. Minneapolis, Minnesota: Augsburg Fortress, 2005.

Luther, Martin. *Luther's works.* Vol. 50, *Letters 3.* Edited by Gottfried G. Krodel. Minneapolis, Minnesota: Fortress Press, 1974.

Russell, William R. *Luther's Theological Testament: The Schmalkald Articles.* Minneapolis, Minnesota: Augsburg Fortress, 1995.